BUSINESS ECONOMICS

ECONOMICS FOR ALL PG AND UG STUDENTS

DR. RAJA KAMAL CH

Made with ♥ on the Notion Press Platform
www.notionpress.com

Dedicated

To

Fr. Josekutty PD

Fr. Dr. Augustine George

Contents

Foreword

This book sets the agenda to turn managerial economics, which has long been considered a subordinate discipline, into mainstream economics. The conceptual and empirical inadequacy of conventional economics using illustrations of real world decision-making in a dynamic environment, including evidence from the global. With a rigorous yet accessible style, they give a comprehensive overview of managerial economics and of the current state of play in the field across different schools of thought. The different concepts of managerial economics are identified and the authors propose to address these issues and allow the discipline to receive its long-awaited recognition.

Crucial reading for students looking for insights into the many concepts of managerial economics.

Preface

This volume of Micro Economics is planned keeping the recent model syllabus of the for B. Com. Fifth Semester course which is common core syllabus for all the universities the basic purpose with which this book has been attempted to present the complex principles of economics in a simple and easy to understand manner. It is our belief that the subject matter in a textbook should be so simple and lucid that students find no problem in understanding them. This is what has been kept in mind while dealing with various topics in this volume. Further, being students of LLB stream, the concepts, principles and techniques of economics are to be dealt with, in a manner so that the students may find them useful in their fields of activities. This is precisely targeted in this book. An important feature of the syllabus is that its coverage is very comprehensive towards dealing with various dimensions of economic analysis. With this perspective in view, the subject matter covers basic branch of micro economics. Given the vastness of the syllabus, special care has been taken not to extend discussion too far beyond the required levels. At the same time, fundamental concepts, thoughts and rationales are made crystal clear with the help of figures and illustrations.

Certain solutions can be objectively provided by economic tools and laws. Economic principles are liberally applied to business issues. A new discipline known as Managerial Economics or Business Economics has emerged in this context, which deals with the application of economic laws to business problems. This new discipline has become a required subject of study in all business programmes at universities.

We hope that the information will be useful to students as they further their education.

It will be a great satisfaction for us, to author as well as to the publisher of this volume, if we have succeeded in our endeavour. The author would like to record his deep sense of thankfulness to the publisher of this volume who has shown full trust in my capabilities and knowledge. However, the errors left despite best efforts will be solely of my responsibility. Being the first edition, there must be scope for improvement. All the constructive suggestions in this regard will be duly acknowledged and appreciated.

Acknowledgements

First and Foremost, thanks to God almighty, the benign, always bestows His divine blessings upon me. I express my humble gratitude to the Omnipotent.

I express my sincere gratitude to Rev. Fr. Josekutty PD, Rev. Fr. Dr. Augustine George, Principal, Fr. Lijo P Thomas, Vice Principal & Chief Finance Officer, Fr. Emmanuel P. J. Director, Kristu Jayanti College of Law, Director, Office of International and Domestic Relations,Jayantian Extension Services & Jayantian Alumni Association, Fr. Som Zacharia, Director, Infrastructure Planning and Development, Fr. Jais V Thomas, Financial Adminstrator, Fr. Joshy Mathew, Director, Library and Information Centre, Director HR Department, Fr. Deepu Joy, Director, Student Welfare Office, Head, Department of English, Dr. Aloysius Edward, Dean and faculty of Commerce & Management and Mr Vijayakumar R, HOD and Faulty members of Kristu Jayanti College who have given valuable support and encouragement throughout my work.

Authors

Prologue

Unit – 1 – Micro Economics and Theory of Consumption

Scope of microeconomics, Limitation and Uses, Positive and Normative economics – Problem of Choice _ wants and resources. Basic economic problems common to all economics, Role of price mechanism in a mixed economy – Cardinal analysis, Law of diminishing marginal utility, Law of equip-marginal utility, consumers surplus (Marshalian) – Ordinal utility analysis indifference curves, properties, map, price line, consumer equilibrium, price effect, income effect and Substitution effect.

Unit – 2 – Demand and Supply

Law of demand, Reasons for the downward slope of demand curve, exception to the law, change in demand – Elasticity of demand, kinds, types of price elasticity demand, factors determining price elasticity of demand, methods of measurement, percentage method, Arc method, total outlay method – Law of supply, changes in supply

Unit – 3 – Theory of Production

Production function, Law of variable proportions, Short run and long run laws of returns, economics to scale, Isoquants, locusts, production equilibrium – Cost, opportunity cost, Real cost, Types, short run, long run, Average, Marginal, Fixed variable, Long run curve – Revenue, Average, Marginal

Unit – 4 – Product Pricing

Concepts of firms, industry, equilibrium - Perfect competition, price and output determination and role of time element in the theory of price determination - Monopoly, price output determination, price discrimination – Monopolistic competition, price and output determination, Selling costs, Product differentiation, Wastes in monopolistic competition – Oligopoly features, Duopoly, Monophony.

Unit – 5 - Factor Pricing

Nature of factor markets, Marginal productivity theory of distribution – Rent, Demand and Supply theory, Quasi rent, Transfer earning – Wages, Reasons for wage differentials, Collective bargaining – Interest, Classical, Neo-classical Keynesian - Profit, Dynamic, Innovation, Risk and Uncertainty theory

1

Microeconomics and Theory of Consumption

Microeconomics and Theory of Consumption

MICRO ECONOMICS

The name "Micro" originates from the Greek word "MIKROS," which translates as "Miniature" or "Millionth part." Microeconomics considers a single customer, a single company, and individual pricing, salaries, and earnings. In other words, it's as if you're peering through a microscope at the economy. Due to the fact that microeconomics focuses only on individual units, Prof. Manson refers to it as a "atomistic individualistic approach."

According to K.E.Boulding micro economics "is the study of particular firms, particular households, individual prices, wages, incomes, individual industries, particular commodities."

In the words of Prof. Mac Canel, "Micro economics is a study of the specific economic units and a detailed consideration of the behaviour of these individual units".

According to Prof. Hansen, "Micro Economics is that branch of economics which is concerned with individual firms, their output and costs, the production and pricing of single commodities, wages of individuals etc."

Thus, microeconomics does not study the economy as a whole but rather as discrete economic units or components. Rather of analysing the forest as a whole, microeconomics considers its constituents. Microeconomics is concerned with resolving three fundamental problems. They are as follows: a) what items are to be produced? b) How will they be manufactured? and c) Whom are they to be created for?

Microeconomics is concerned with the following topics: I commodity pricing, ii) factor pricing, and iii) welfare economics. The significance of microeconomics.

Microeconomics has a significant deal of practical value. The following are the advantages of this strategy:

1. The economy's operation:

Microeconomic analysis enables us to comprehend the operation of a complex economic system.

2. Economic policy formulation:

Microeconomics equips policymakers with the essential tools. Microstudies-based policies are more effective and relevant.

3. Economic welfare research:

Microeconomics is extremely useful in examining economic wellbeing circumstances. Microeconomics enables us to comprehend the standard of living of individuals, their welfare status, their degree of contentment, and the factors that influence wellbeing, among other things.

4. Resource allocation: Microeconomics is extremely beneficial in allocating scarce productive resources among various purposes. It enables resource allocation and use to be more efficient.

5. Economic theory formulation:

Microeconomics is extremely beneficial in developing several economic theories and generalizations. To develop viable economic theories, the economic theorist must have a working grasp of microeconomics.

6. Taxation analysis:

Microeconomics is quite beneficial for comprehending the implications of taxation. It is necessary for the development of tax policy.

Limitations of microeconomics:

Micro economics suffers from certain limitations. Following are its main defects.

1. Irresponsible assumptions:

Microeconomics is predicated on a number of implausible assumptions, including full employment, perfect competition, and a laissez-faire policy.

2. Deceptive:

Microeconomics can be deceptive at times. Because what applies to a person may not apply to an economy. Occasionally, generalisations based on micro studies lead to incorrect conclusions.

3. There is no clear picture:

Microeconomic analysis will not provide a comprehensive view of the economy. This is because it will not address the economy as a whole.

4. Limited scope: Microeconomics is a rather narrow field of study. It appears insufficient to account for the economy's behaviour.

Microeconomics, in this sense, has several flaws. Despite these restrictions, it is extremely beneficial to understand how an economic system works. Because microeconomics deals with the distribution of products and resources among various purposes, it is referred to as the pricing theory.

POSITIVE ECONOMICS AND NORMATIVE ECONOMICS

Economic science is either a positive or a normative science. This is by far the most contentious issue in economics. Among economists themselves, there is no unanimity. According to some, economics is a positive science. According to some, it is a normative science. However, many others regard it as both. To determine if economics is a positive or normative science, one must first understand what they are.

Positive science elucidates the origins and effects of events. It examines facts as they are, not as they should be. A positive science is one that only investigates and explains. As such, it is more illuminating; it conducts a critical investigation of existing data and draws conclusions.

Additionally, economics is a positive science. Because it examines not just the causes but also the repercussions of numerous events. For instance, it investigates the origins of economic inequality, unemployment, and poverty, as well as their societal consequences. Prof. Robbins, Nassau senior, and other English economists believe that economics is a positive science that should be free of ethical constraints.

In contrast, economists such as R.G. Hawtrey, Fraser, and Thomas, among others, believe that economics is a normative science. A normative science is concerned with the correctness or incorrectness of things. It examines things as they should be. It is not simply a source of light, but also a source of 'fruit'. A normative science not only investigates and explains, but also imposes ethical standards of behaviour. It is not a neutral medium between goals, but positive science is.

Economics is a normative science in that it not only examines the origins and effects of economic disparity, poverty, and unemployment, but also demonstrates why these inequalities are socially unjustifiable. Thus, it informs us about the things as they are and as they should be.

Numerous economists believe that economics is both a positive and normative science. They believe that economics' positive and normative perspectives should coexist. An economist's role is not simply to watch and analyse, but also to advise. Occasionally, economists must make value judgments, and economics cannot be divorced from ethics. Thus, economics is a positive as well as a normative science.

BASIC PROBLEMS OF AN ECONOMY

While human desires are limitless, resources are not. Individuals and society are forced to make choices due to limited or restricted resources. This issue of choice has spawned an economic crisis, which must be resolved.

(A) AN ECONOMY'S MEANING

An economy or economic system refers to the factors that govern the production and distribution of commodities and services in a country. Additionally, it refers to the way in which individuals earn a living. In other terms, the term 'economy' refers to all sources of employment and output within a certain geographical region. It is comprised of all persons, homes, groups, businesses, industries, banks, and government entities that operate and interact in order to generate and consume products and services.

Thus, an economy is a social organism that provides a means of subsistence for individuals. It refers to a country's organisation of economic activities such as production, consumption, exchange, and distribution of products and services. It demonstrates how a country's citizens earn a living by coordinating numerous forms of activity. Today, the globe is home to a variety of economies and economic systems. For instance, we discuss the Indian economy, the Japanese economy, the United States economy, and the Pakistani economy, among others.

How does an economy function?

A contemporary economy's operation is exceedingly complex and intricate. Thousands of individuals join and contribute to its operation in a variety of ways and abilities. They are employed as producers, employees, customers, merchants, financiers, administrators, educators, attorneys, and social workers, among other positions. Thousands of goods and services are manufactured and consumed here, and thousands of people work in the manufacturing and distribution of these goods and services.

Economic actions of various people are interconnected and interdependent in a contemporary economy. Their relationship, collaboration, and competitiveness all reflect this. In a simplified model of a contemporary economy, the economic actors are grouped as follows: I households, (ii) business firms, and (iii) the government. Households contribute in the economy in two distinct ways. They operate as producers of productive resources, such as land, labour, and capital, as well as consumers of commodities and services created. Businesses manufacture and distribute goods and services. The government is the third critical component in the contemporary economy. It collects taxes from individuals and businesses and provides a variety of products and services to the public. Additionally, it supervises, regulates, and directs people's economic activity in order to accomplish particular social and economic goals.

(B) ESSENTIAL ECONOMICAL PROBLEMS

The primary issue confronting an economy is 'economising on restricted resources.' The problem of scarcity arose as a result of insatiable desires and finite resources. This is true of all types of economies - developed and developing, wealthy and impoverished. The disparity between desires and resources created the problem of choice, or the task of determining other uses for finite resources. If an economy has an infinite number of desires and an equally infinite number of resources to satisfy them, there will be no economic difficulty. This is not the case, though. As a result, any economy, whether capitalist, socialist, or hybrid, must confront the following fundamental economic difficulties.

(i) What to produce? (Problem of choice) The first central problem of an economy is to decide what to

Produce and the quantity that should be produced. The dilemma of 'what to create' is a decision between goods, and it arose as a result of resource scarcity. The difficulty of determining the quantity of each item and service to be produced is referred to as the "how much to produce" question. This issue also occurred as a result of resource shortage. The challenge of what to create and how much to produce is ultimately a matter of allocating finite resources efficiently between conflicting requirements. The purpose of an economy should be to maximise output in order to meet the biggest number of people's needs. Thus, each economy is forced to choose between a variety of commodities and services due to the scarcity or limitation of available resources.

(ii) How to produce? (Problem of choice of technique)

The economy's next challenge is determining how to generate products and services. This issue of 'how to create' is a matter of technique selection. This issue also occurred as a result of resource shortage. Given the scarcity of resources, it becomes vital to select a technology that maximises resource use. The challenge of how to produce entails determining I what resources and technology should be used to make the things, (ii) the size at which the goods should be produced, and (iii) the sector in which the goods should be produced. There are several different production processes, and the economy must select one. Additionally, commodities may be manufactured employing a variety of different resources in varying amounts. Depending on the availability of resources, the economy must decide how to combine various resources. It must also determine whether to produce on a large or small scale, in the private or public sector.

(iii) For whom to produce? (Problem of distribution)

The third fundamental issue confronting an economy is determining for whom the goods will be produced. This is an issue with the distribution of commodities and services among society's members. In other words, determining 'for whom to create' entails deciding how the generated items will be allocated among the many individuals and families in society. It is concerned with the distribution of national product among distinct functional groupings or production elements. The answer to this challenge will be determined in large part by the kind and type of economic system in place. The distribution of products in a capitalist economy is governed by customer preferences and pricing mechanisms. It is determined by the central planning authority in a socialist economy.

Finally, the economy must determine whether its resources are being fully utilised and whether it is expanding or stagnating.

Consumer Behavior

Meaning

Consumer behavior is the study of how individual customers, groups, or organizations select, buy, use, and dispose of ideas, goods, and services to satisfy their needs and wants. It refers to the actions of the consumers in the marketplace and the underlying motives for those actions.

Approaches to the Study of Consumer Behavior

The theory of consumer behaviour aims to explain how consumer equilibrium is determined. Consumer equilibrium refers to the state in which a consumer obtains the greatest amount of satisfaction from his available resources. A customer spends his money income on a variety of items and services in order to maximise his enjoyment. Once a customer achieves equilibrium, he is averse to deviating from it.

Economic theory has handled the challenge of determining the equilibrium of consumers in two distinct ways:

1. Cardinal Utility Analysis and (2) Ordinal Utility Analysis Accordingly,

We shall examine these two approaches to the study of consumer's equilibrium in greater deficit.

Cardinal approach – Law of Diminishing Marginal Utility

Utility Analysis or Cardinal Approach:

The Cardinal Approach to consumer behaviour theory is predicated on the idea of utility. It presupposes that utility can be quantified. It can be added to, subtracted from, or multiplied, among other operations.

A benefit may be quantified using cardinal numbers such as 1,2,3,4, etc. Fisher used the term 'Utile' to refer to a unit of utility. Thus, in terms of the cardinal method, one obtains 5 utiles from a cup of tea, 10 utiles from a cup of coffee, and 15 utiles from a rasagulla.

Meaning of Utility:

In economics, the term utility refers to the quality of an item or service that satisfies our desires. In other terms, utility is defined as a commodity's capacity to satisfy desires.

According to, Mrs. Robinson, "Utility is the quality in commodities that makes individuals want to buy them."

According to Hibdon, "Utility is the quality of a good to satisfy a want." Law of Diminishing

Law of Diminishing Marginal Utility

Introduction

The law of declining marginal value is critical to comprehend. Although it belongs under the subject of Microeconomics, it plays an equal and substantial role in our daily decisions.

Meaning

Alfred Marshall provides a thorough explanation of the law of declining marginal value. According to his explanation of the law of declining marginal utility, "when more units of a commodity are consumed, each consecutive unit provides utility at a diminishing rate, given that other variables remain constant; yet, overall utility grows."

"With all other variables being constant, when an individual purchases successive units of an item, the marginal utility declines continuously."

The marginal utility of a good decreases when the user acquires more of it. Marginal utility is the change in overall utility caused by a unit change in a commodity's consumption per unit of time.

The explanation for the Law of Diminishing Marginal Utility:

With the use of an example, we may succinctly illustrate Marshall's thesis. Assume that a client consumes six apples consecutively. The first apple provides him with twenty utils (units for measuring utility). When he swallows the second and third apples, the marginal utility of each subsequent apple decreases. This is because as apple consumption increases, his desire to consume more apples decreases.

As a result, this example demonstrates that each subsequent unit of a product utilised diminishes the usefulness.

With the use of a timetable and diagram, we can illustrate this point more clearly.

Schedule for Law of Diminishing Marginal Utility:

Unit of Consumption	Marginal Utility	Total Utility
1	20	20
2	15	35
3	10	45
4	05	50
5	00	50
6	-05	45

Table: Schedule for Law of Diminishing Marginal Utility

The overall utility acquired from the first apple is 20 utilitarian, and this value continues to increase until we hit our saturation point at the fifth apple. On the other hand, marginal utility continues to decline when more apples are consumed. We exceeded the limit when we consumed the sixth apple. As a result, marginal utility is negative and total utility decreases.

With the help of the schedule, we have made the following diagram:

Marginal Utility curve

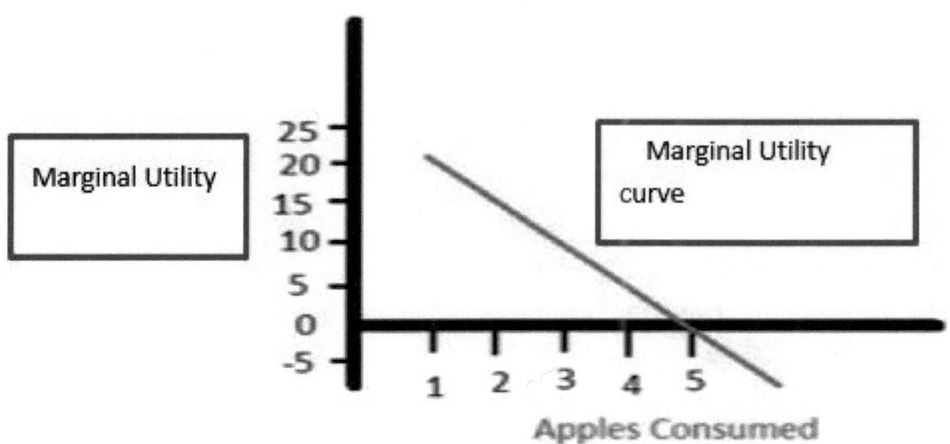

Fig: Marginal Utility Curve

Saturation Point: The moment at which the urge to eat the same thing vanishes.

Disutility: If you continue to consume the product after it reaches its saturation threshold, the total usefulness decreases. This is referred to as a disutility.

The marginal value of the first apple ingested is twenty. When the second apple is consumed, the marginal utility improves by 15 useful units, but is still less than the marginal utility of the first apple — due to the declining rate. As a result, we have demonstrated that the usefulness of apples ingested decreases as the quantity consumed increases.

Similarly, after the fifth apple, we have reached our saturation point. When we devour another apple, the marginal utility curve falls below the X-axis, which is referred to as 'disutility'.

Assumptions:

Following are the assumptions of the law of diminishing marginal utility.

1. Utility is quantifiable, and an individual may describe the utility gained from a product in qualitative terms such as two units, four units, or seven units, and so on.
2. A rational consumer's objective is to maximise his utility.
3. A constant unit of measurement must exist for a standard unit of measurement.
4. A commodity is continually consumed. Any difference between the consumption of an item and its production should be appropriate.
5. Appropriate units of an item consumed by the consumer should exist.
6. It is believed that the features of distinct commodity units are homogeneous.
7. The consumer's taste stays consistent during the intake of successive units of the product.
8. During the operation of the law of declining marginal utility, the consumer's income stays constant.
9. The commodity is supposed to be divisible.
10. Fashion should remain constant. For instance, if a fashion trend favours raised shirts, the buyer may see little use in exposed shirts.

Exceptions or Limitations:

The limitations or exceptions of the law of diminishing marginal utility are as follows:

1. The legislation is unconvincing in the case of rare collections. For instance, a collection of old coins, stamps, or other collectibles.
2. The legislation does not apply entirely to money. Money's marginal utility decreases with wealth but never reaches zero.
3. It excludes knowledge, art, and invention.
4. The legislation does not apply to valuable commodities.
5. Exceptions to the statute include historical items.
6. The law is ineffective if the customer acts unreasonably. For instance, it is stated that the alcoholic enjoys each succeeding peg more than the preceding one.
7. Man is a lover of beauty and ornamentation. He obtains more happiness by acquiring the items' above-mentioned virtues.
8. When a clothing becomes fashionable, its functionality increases. On the other side, if it becomes out of style, its utility decreases.
9. The demonstration boosts the utility. It is a naturally occurring element.

Importance of the Law of Diminishing Marginal Utility:

The importance or the role of the law of diminishing marginal utility is as follows:

1. When more of a commodity is purchased, the marginal utility drops. As a result of this conduct, the customer reduces his spending on that product.
2. This law has a practical application in the realm of public finance, inflicting a larger cost on the wealthy.
3. This rule serves as the foundation for several other economic laws, including the law of demand, the law of demand elasticity, consumer surplus, and the law of substitution, among others.
4. A commodity's value decreases as its supply is increased. It serves as the foundation for value theory. This is how prices are established.

Law of Equi-Marginal Utility

H. H. Gossen, an Australian economist, introduced the law of eqi marginal utility in the nineteenth century. It is also known as Gossen's second law, the law of maximum satisfaction, the law of substitution, or the rule of substitution. A consumer has a variety of desires. He attempts to allocate his limited money among various activities in such a manner that the marginal value of all activities is equal. When he purchases several items with a given amount of money, he equalises the marginal utility of all such items. The law of equal marginal utility is a generalisation of the declining marginal utility rule. Maximum utility is obtained by distributing income across commodities in such a way that the final dollar spent on each item offers the same marginal utility.

Definition:

"A person can get maximum utility with his given income when it is spent on different commodities in such a way that the marginal utility of money spent on each item is equal".

The consumer can get maximum utility from the expenditure of his limited income. He should purchase such amount of each commodity that the last unit of money spend on each item provides the same marginal utility.

Assumptions of the Law of Equi Marginal Utility:

1. There is no change in the prices of the goods.
2. The income of the consumer is fixed.
3. The marginal utility of money is constant.
4. The consumer has perfect knowledge of utility obtained from goods.
5. A consumer is a normal person so he tries to seek maximum satisfaction.
6. The utility is measurable in cardinal terms.
7. The consumer has many wants.
8. The goods have substitutes.

Explanation With Schedule and Diagram:

The law of substitution can be explained with the help of an example. Suppose the consumer has six dollars that he wants to spend on apples and bananas to obtain maximum total utility. The following table shows the marginal utility (MU) of spending additional dollars of income on apples and bananas:

Money (Units)	MU of apples	MU of bananas
1	10	8
2	9	7
3	8	6
4	7	5
5	6	4
6	5	3

Table: Schedule of Law of Equi-Marginal Utility

The above schedule shows that consumers can spend six dollars in different ways:

1. ?1 on apples and ?5 on bananas. The total utility he can get is:
   [(10) + (8+7+6+5+4)] = 40.
2. ?2 on apples and ?4 on bananas. The total utility he can get is:
   [(10+9) + (8+7+6+5)] = 45.
3. ?3 on apples and ?3 on bananas. The total utility he can get is:
   [(10+9+8) + (8+7+6)] = 48.

4. ?4 on apples and ?2 on bananas. This way the total utility is:
   [(10+9+8+7) + (8+7)] = 49.
5. ?5 on apples and ?1 on bananas. The total utility he can get is:
   [(10+9+8+7+6) + (8)] = 48.

The total utility for the consumer is 49 utils that is the highest obtainable with the expenditure of ?4 on apples and ?2 on bananas. Here the condition MU of apple = MU of banana i.e 7 = 7 is also satisfied. Any other allocation of the last dollar shall give less total utility to the consumer.

The same information can be used for the Graphical presentation of this law:

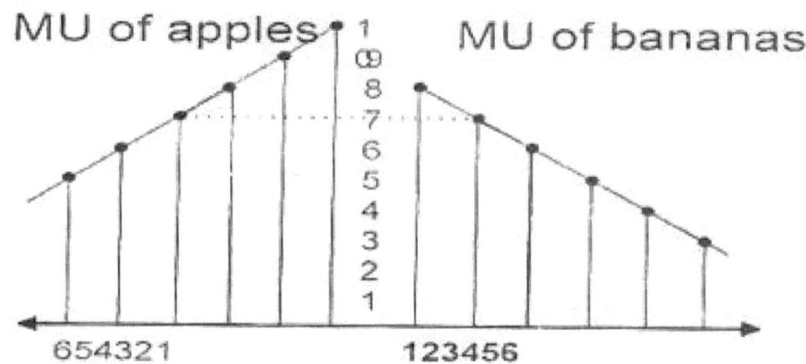

Fig: Law of Equi-Marginal Utility

The diagram shows that the consumer has an income of six dollars. He wants to spend this money on apples and bananas in such a way that there is maximum satisfaction to the consumer.

Limitations:

1. The law is not applicable in the case of knowledge. Reading books provides more satisfaction and knowledge to the scholar. Different books provide a variety of knowledge and satisfaction.
2. The law is not applicable in the case of indivisible goods. The consumer is unable to divide the goods to adjust units of utility derived from the consumption of goods.
3. There is no measurement of utility. It is a psychological concept. It is not possible to express it in quantitative form.
4. The law does not hold well in case fashion and customs. People like to spend money on birthdays, marriages, and deaths.
5. The does not hold well in the case of very low income. The maximization of utility is not possible due to low income.
6. The law is not applicable in the case of durable goods. The calculation of marginal utility of durable goods is impossible.
7. The law fails when goods of choice are not available. The consumer is bound to use commodity, which provides low utility due to the non-availability of goods having high utility.
8. There are certain lazy consumers. They do not care for maximum utility. The law fails to operate in case of laziness of consumers. They go on consuming goods with comparing utility.
9. It does not work when there are frequent prices changes. The consumer is unable to calculate the utility of different commodities. Changing price levels create confusion in the minds of consumers.
10. There may be unlimited resources. The does not work due to unlimited resources. There is no need to change the direction of expenditure from one item to another when there are gifts of nature.

Importance:

1. The law of equi marginal utility is helpful in the field of production. The producer has limited resources. He uses limited resources to purchase production factors. He tries to equalize the marginal utility of all factors. He wishes to get maximum output and profit.
2. National income is distributed among factors of production according to this law. An entrepreneur can pay factors of production equal to marginal product measured in money terms. He will substitute one factor for another until marginal productivity of all factors is equal to the prices of their services.
3. The law is used in the field of exchange. The people like to exchange a commodity having low utility with a commodity having high utility. There is maximum benefit from the exchange of commodities. The law is helpful in the exchange of wealth, trade, import, and export.
4. The law is applicable in consumption. A rational consumer tries to get maximum satisfaction when he spends his limited resources on various things. He tries to equalize the weighted marginal utility of all things.
5. The law is applicable in public finance. The government can spend its revenue to get the maximum social advantage. The marginal utility of each dollar spent in one sector must be equal to the marginal utility derived from all other sectors.
6. The law is useful for workers in allocating the time between work and rest. They can compare the marginal utility of work and the marginal utility of rest. They can decide working hours and rest hours.
7. The law holds well in the case of saving and spending. The consumer can choose between present wants and future wants. He can feel that a dollar saved has greater utility than a dollar spent, he can save more and spend less. He will substitute saving and spending till the marginal utility of a dollar spent and a dollar saved are equal.
8. The law is helpful in prices. Due to the scarcity of commodities its prices go up. The law tells us to use substitute commodity, which is less scarce. The result is that the price of a commodity comes down.

Consumer Surplus

Introduction to Consumer Surplus:

The doctrine of Consumer's Surplus which occupies an important place in the Marshallian System of Welfare Economic Analysis was originally stated by William Stanley Jevons and French Engineer economist Arsen's Jules Dupuit in 1844 in a Crude form.

Later on, Dr. Alfred Marshall explained this concept in "The Pure Theory of Domestic Values" as consumer's rent. In his 'Principles of Economics,' he further elaborated this concept in logical detail and describe it as "Consumer's Surplus". He is called the Consumer's Surplus.

Definition of Consumer Surplus:

1. **Regarding this Prof. Marshall** has said that "The excess of price which he (consumer) would be willing to pay rather than go without. The thing over that which he does pay, is the economic measure of this surplus satisfaction. It may be called "Consumer's Surplus".

2. **According to Penson** – "The difference between what we would pay and what we have to pay is called Consumer's Surplus."

3. **According to Prof. J. K. Mehta** – "Consumer's Surplus obtained by a person from a commodity is the difference between satisfaction which he derives from it and which he foregoes to procure that commodity."

4. **As per Samuelson** – "There is always a gap between total welfare and total economic value. This gap is the nature of a surplus which consumer gets because he always receives more than he pays."

5. **According to Taussig** – "Consumer's Surplus is the difference between the sum which measures total exchange value".

Importance of Consumer's Surplus:

The concept of consumer surplus has both theoretical as well as practical importance.

(i) Theoretical importance: The idea of consumer surplus reveals the benefits which we derive from our purchase of the commodity in the market.

For example, when we purchase salt or a matchbox, we are willing to pay an amount much higher than their market value. For example, a consumer would be willing to pay ?10 for a matchbox rather than go without it but he pays Re one only on the purchase of a matchbox. Consumer's surplus on the purchase of matchbox thus is ? 9.0.

(ii) Practical importance: A monopolist can charge a higher price for his product if the consumers are enjoying a large consumers surplus on the use of his product.

(iii) The inhabitants of a country derive consumer surplus when they import commodities from abroad. They are usually prepared to pay more for what they pay.

(iv) A finance minister imposes taxes on the commodities yielding consumer surplus.

(v) An entrepreneur before investing capital in a project evaluates the consumer's surplus to be derived from it. If the benefits to the obtained are greater than the costs, the investment is undertaken.

Ordinal Utility Approach

The basic idea behind the **ordinal utility approach** is that a consumer keeps the number of pairs of two commodities in his mind which gives him an equal level of satisfaction. This means that the utility can be ranked qualitatively.

The ordinal theory is also known as the neo-classical theory of consumer equilibrium, **Hicksian** theory of consumer behavior, indifference curve theory, optimal choice theory. This approach also explains the consumer's equilibrium who is confronted with the multiplicity of objectives and scarcity of money income.

The important tools of ordinal utility are:

1. The concept of indifference curves.
2. The slop of I.C. i.e. marginal rate of substitution.
3. The budget line.

Assumptions:

The ordinal utility approach is based on the following assumptions:

1. A consumer substitutes commodities rationally to maximize his level of satisfaction.
2. A consumer can rank his preferences according to the satisfaction of each basket of goods.
3. The consumer is consistent in his choices.
4. It is assumed that each of the goods is divisible.
5. It is assumed that the consumer has full knowledge of prices in the market.
6. The consumer's scale of preferences is so complete that the consumer is indifferent between them.
7. Two commodities are used by the consumer. It is also known as the two commodities model.
8. Two commodities X and Y are substitutes for each other. These commodities can be easily substituted in various pairs.

Theory of Indifference Curve Analysis

Definition and Explanation:

The ***indifference curve*** indicates the various combinations of two goods that yield equal satisfaction to the consumer.

By definition: "An indifference curve shows all the various combinations of two goods that give an equal amount of satisfaction to a consumer".

Assumptions: The ***indifference curve analysis*** is based on four main assumptions.

(i) Rational behavior of the consumer: It is assumed that individuals are rational in making decisions from their expenditures on consumer goods.

(ii) Utility is ordinal: Utility cannot be measured cardinally. It can be, however, expressed ordinally. In other words, the consumer can rank the basket of goods according to the satisfaction or utility of each basket.

(iii) Diminishing marginal rate of substitution: In the indifference curve analysis, the principle of diminishing marginal rate of substitution is assumed.

(iv) Consistency in choice: The consumer, it is assumed, is consistent in his behavior during a period. For insistence, if the consumer prefers combinations of A of good to the combinations B of goods, he then remains consistent in his choice. His preference, during another period, does not change. Symbolically, it can be expressed as:

If A > B, then B > A

(iv) Consumer's preference not self-contradictory: The consumer's preferences are not self-contradictory. It means that if combination A is preferred over combination B is preferred over C, then combination A is preferred over combination A is preferred over C. Symbolically it can be expressed:

If A > B and B > C, then A > C

(v) Goods consumed are substitutable: The goods consumed by the consumer are substitutable. The utility can be maintained at the same level by consuming more of some goods and less of the other. There are many combinations of the two commodities which are equally preferred by a consumer and he is indifferent as to which of the two he receives.

Indifference curve analysis

It is a curve that represents all the combinations of goods that give the same satisfaction to the consumer. Since all the combinations give the same amount of satisfaction, the consumer prefers them equally. Hence the name Indifference Curve.

Here is an example to understand the indifference curve better. Peter has 1 unit of food and 12 units of clothing. Now, we ask Peter how many units of clothing is he willing to give up in exchange for an additional unit of food so that his level of satisfaction remains unchanged.

Peter agrees to give up 6 units of clothing for an additional unit of food. Hence, we have two combinations of food and clothing giving equal satisfaction to Peter as follows:

1. 1 unit of food and 12 units of clothing
2. 2 units of food and 6 units of clothing

By asking him similar questions, we get various combinations as follows:

Indifference Curve Schedule:

Combination	Food	Clothing
A	1	12
B	2	6
C	3	4
D	4	3

Table: Indifference Curve Schedule

Graphical Representation:

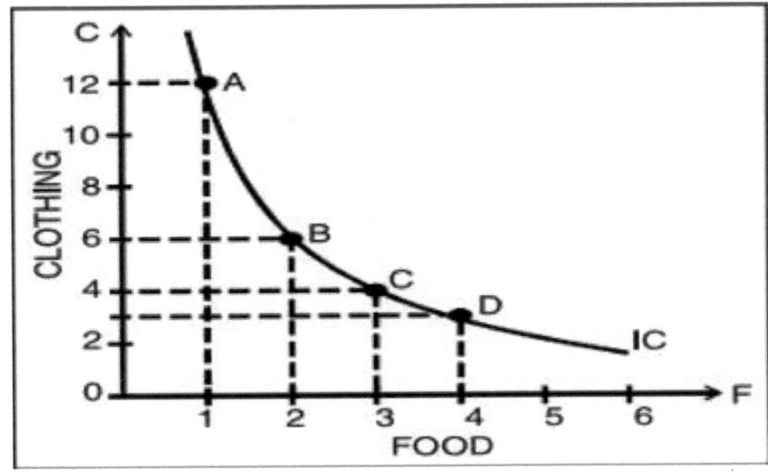

Fig: Indifference curve

The Fig 1 shows an Indifference curve (IC). Any combination lying on this curve gives the same level of consumer satisfaction. It is also known as Iso-Utility Curve.

Indifference Map

An Indifference Map is a set of Indifference Curves. It depicts the complete picture of a consumer's preferences. The Fig 2 showing an indifference map consisting of three curves:

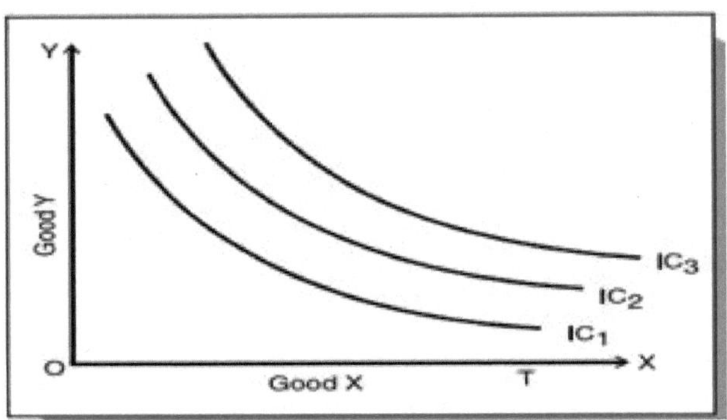

Fig: Indifference Map

We know that a consumer is indifferent among the combinations lying on the same indifference curve. However, it is important to note that he prefers the combinations on the higher indifference curves to those on the lower ones.

This is because a higher indifference curve implies a higher level of satisfaction. Therefore, all combinations on IC1 offer the same satisfaction, but all combinations on IC2 give greater satisfaction than those on IC1.

Marginal Rate of Substitution

This is the rate at which a consumer is prepared to exchange a good X for Y. If we go back to Peter's example above, we have the following table:

Combination	Food	Clothing	MRS
A	1	12	-
B	2	6	6
C	3	4	2
D	4	3	1

Table: Marginal Rate of Substitution

In this example, Peter initially gives up 6 units of clothing to get an extra unit of food. Hence, the MRS is 6. Similarly, for subsequent exchanges, the MRS is 2 and 1 respectively. Therefore, the MRS of X for Y is the amount of Y whose loss can be compensated by a unit gain of X, keeping the satisfaction the same.

Interestingly, as Peter accumulates more units of food, the MRS starts falling – meaning he is prepared to give up fewer units of clothing for food. There are two reasons for this:

1. As Peter gets more units of food, his intensity of desire for additional units of food decreases.
2. Most of the goods are imperfect substitutes for one another. If they could substitute one another perfectly, then MRS would remain constant.

Properties of indifference curve

There are four basic properties of an indifference curve. These properties are

The indifference curve slopes downwards to the right

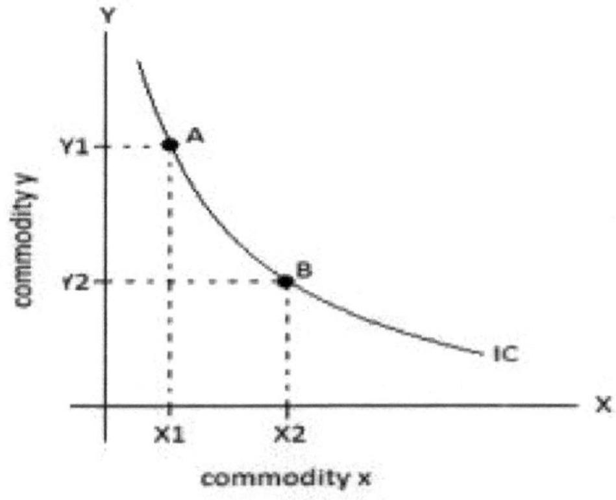

Fig: Curve Slopes Downwards

An indifference curve can neither be a horizontal line nor an upward sloping curve. This is an important feature of an indifference curve.

When a consumer wants to have more of a commodity, he/she will have to give up some of the other commodities, given that the consumer remains on the same level of utility at constant income. As a result, the indifference curve slopes downward from left to right.

Indifference curve is always convex (neither concave nor straight).

Due to the diminishing marginal rate of substitution. The rate gives a convex shape to the indifference curve, always indifference curve is convex shape neither concave nor straight

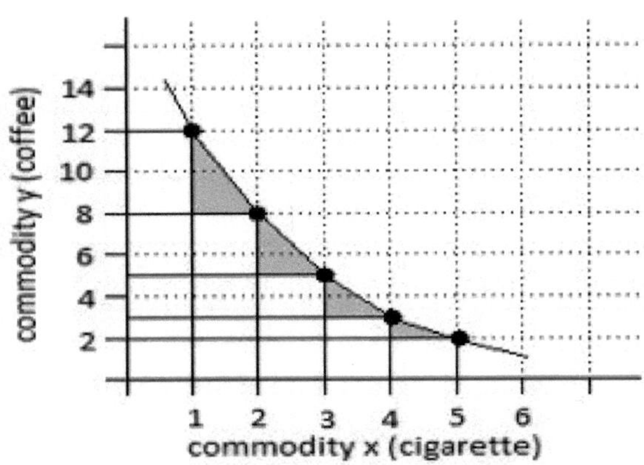

Fig: Convex Cuve

Indifference curves cannot intersect each other

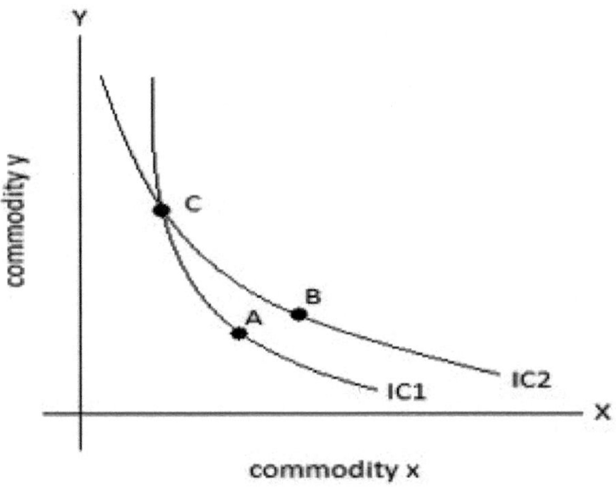

Fig: Curves with intersection

Each indifference curve is a representation of a particular level of satisfaction. The level of satisfaction of consumers for any given combination of two commodities is the same for a consumer throughout the curve. Thus, indifference curves cannot intersect each other.

A higher indifference curve represents a higher level of satisfaction

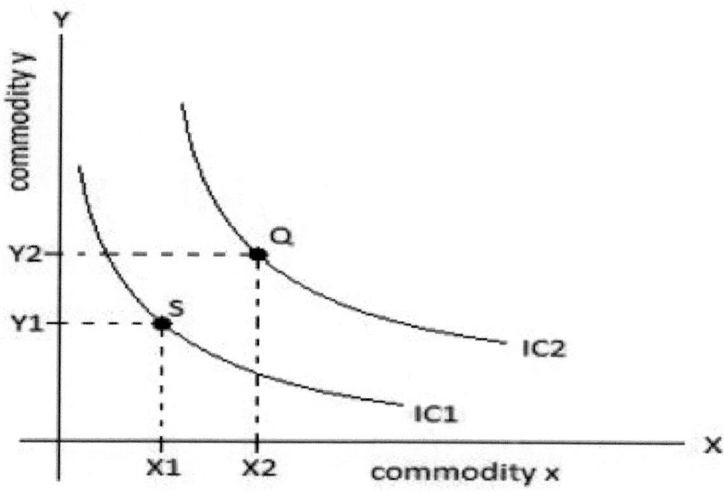

Fig: Higher level of satisfaction curve

The higher the indifference curves, the higher will be the level of satisfaction. This means any combination of two goods on the higher curve gives a higher level of satisfaction to the consumer than the combination of goods on the lower curve.

2

Demand and Supply

Demand and Supply

MEANING OF DEMAND

Introduction

Ordinarily, demand means the desire or wants for something. In Economics, however, demand means much more than that. The Economics meaning of demand refers to the effective date and, i.e., the quantity the buyers are willing to purchase at a given price and over a given period. This concept of demand may be looked upon as follows:

1. Demand is the desire or want back up money

Demand means effective desire or wants for a commodity, which is backed up by the ability and willingness to pay for it. Demand = Desire + Ability to pay (money or purchasing power) + Will to spend.

2. Demand is always related to price and time

Demand is not an absolute term. It is a relative concept. Demand for a commodity should always have a reference to price and time. Economists always mention the amount of demand for a commodity concerning a particular price and specific periods, such as per day, per week, per month, or year.

Definition of demand: the demand for a product refers to the amount of it which will be bought per unit of time at a particular price.

3. Demand may be viewed ex-ante or ex-post

Demand for a commodity may be viewed as ex-ante i.e., intended demand, or ex-post i.e., what is already purchased. The former denotes potential demand while the latter refers to the actual amount purchased.

Demand in economics is the consumer's desire and ability to purchase a good or service. It's the underlying force that drives economic growth and expansion. Without demand, no business would ever bother producing anything.

Determinants of Demand

Introduction: The demand for a product is influenced by several factors. An organization should properly understand the relationship between the demand and each determinant to analyze and estimate the individual and market demand of a product. The demand for a product is influenced by various factors, such as price, consumer's income, and growth of population.

For example, the demand for apparel changes with changes in fashion and the tastes and preferences of consumers. The extent to which these factors influence demand depends on the nature of a product.

An organization, while analyzing the effect of one particular determinant on demand, needs to assume other determinants to be constant. This is because if all the determinants are allowed to differ simultaneously, then it would be difficult to estimate the extent of change in demand.

Following are the determinants of demand for a product:

Determinant 1. Price of the Commodity:

The price of the commodity is the most important determinant of the demand. As it is well known, there is an inverse relationship between the price of a product and its demand. That is, a fall in the price of the product will increase demand by a buyer and vice versa. More on this relationship is explained under the law of demand.

Determinant 2. Prices of Related Goods:

Another variable of high significance is the prices of the related goods, which may be a substitute or a complement. They are collectively known as related goods.

Determinant 3. Substitute Goods:

A substitute is a good that can be used in place of a particular good as it provides the same kind of utility. For example, a train ride is a substitute for a bus ride; a pear for an apple and, a gel pen for a ball pen. If the price of a substitute increases and the price level of the product remains the same then the demand for the product will rise as it will become relatively cheaper.

To explain this, let us presume that the price of the product X and its substitute is equal to Rs.4 per unit, to begin with. So, the sum required to procure,

1 unit of product X = 1 unit of substitute

Subsequently, the price of substitutes doubles to Rs.8 per unit. Now, for the consumer,

2 units of product X = 1 unit of substitute

This implies that product X has become relatively cheaper vis-a-vis its substitute. This will increase the demand for product X despite no change in its price.

It means that the price of a substitute and the demand of a given product move in the same direction. That is, if the price of a substitute increases, the demand for the given product will increase and vice versa. This is shown graphically in Figure by an upward-looking positively sloped curve AB.

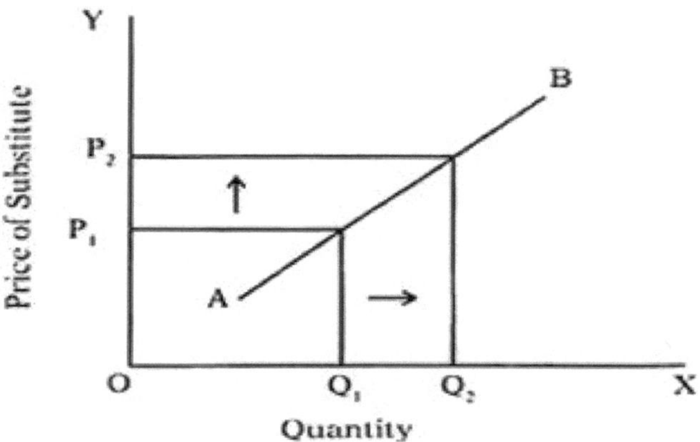

Fig: Positive sloped curve

In the case of gel pens and ball pens, for instance, if the price of gel pens increases then the demand for ball pens will increase. Conversely, if the price of a substitute (gel pen) decreases, the demand for the product (ball pen) will also decrease.

This happens because an increase in the price of substitutes will make the product relatively cheaper and the buyer will demand cheaper goods than its expensive substitutes. Similarly, if the price of substitute falls, it will make the product expensive vis-a-vis its substitute and, hence, its demand will fall.

Further, the effect of change in the price of a substitute occurs no matter what is the price of the product. As a consequence, a change in the price of the substitute will change the entire demand schedule and causes the demand curve of the product to shift, as shown in Figure The figure shows that an increase in the price of the substitute will lead the demand curve of the product to shift upward while a fall in the price of the substitute leads its demand curve to shift downwards.

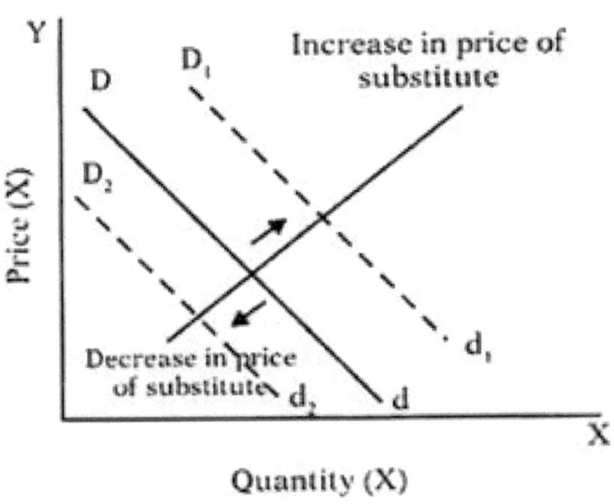

Fig: Curve shifting downwards

Determinant 4. Complement Goods:

A complement is a commodity that has to be used in conjunction with the given commodity. For example, petrol and car, bricks and cement, ink-pen and ink are to be consumed jointly. This property of consumption implies that if one of them becomes expensive the demand for the other will decrease and vice versa.

An increase in the price of ink, for example, will reduce the demand for ink-pen. In nutshell, the demand of a product is inversely related to the price of its complement, as shown by a negatively sloped demand curve AB in Figure.

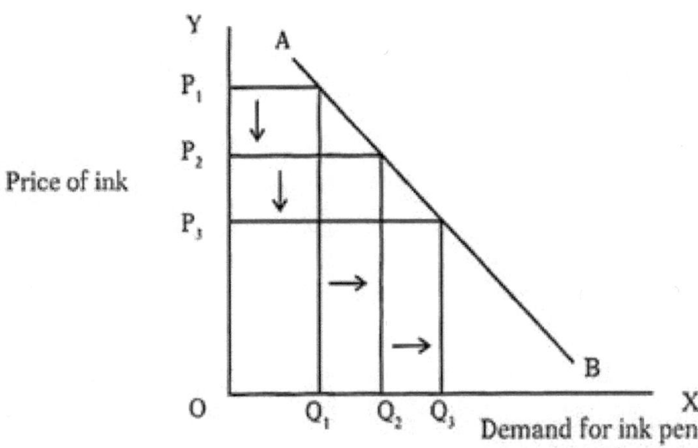

Fig: Negitively sloped

Determinant 5. Income of the Consumer:

A buyer's income is another important determinant of the demand for a product. It represents the purchasing power of the buyer. When income increases, buyer demands more of normal goods and vice versa. There is, thus, a direct relationship between income and demand for a normal or superior good.

Figure(a), shows an upward shift in the demand curve of normal goods when income rises and a downward shift when it falls. An upward shift in the demand curve will show that at each given price consumers will demand more of the product at higher income. Similarly, a downward shift in the demand curve will mean a fall in demand on each price when the income of the buyer falls.

The behavior of inferior goods will be the just reverse of normal goods. The demand for an inferior product will fall as the income of the buyer rises and vice versa. Such behavior is exhibited in Figure (b)

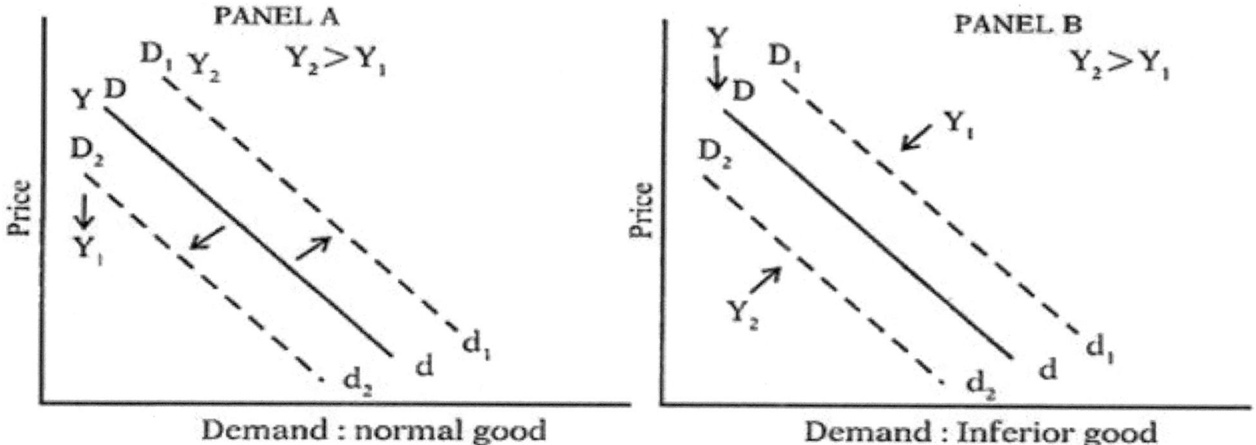

Fig(a): Normal Good Fig(b): Inferior Good

In Figure(a), at income level Y, the price-quantity relationship is exhibited by the demand curve Dd. When income rises to Y_2, the demand curve moves upward and assumes the position at D_1d_1. Thus, at each price level, the expected demand of the product will be more at income level than the Y_2 than that of at income level Y. Similarly, when income falls to Y_1 from Y, the demand curve moves downwards and assumes the position at D_2d_2. As a result, demand will be less at each possible price level.

However, the inferior and Giffen goods will not behave in this fashion. Their demand will fall as the income rises, as shown in Figure(b). When income rises from Y to Y_2, the demand curve has shifted downward to D_2d_2 and when income falls from Y to Y_1, it shifted to D_1d_1. An upward shift in the demand curve will mean more demand at the same price and vice versa.

It also implies higher demand for inferior goods when income falls and lower demand when income rises, the price remains the same. This happens because the consumer will move on to some superior product as his buying power increases and, therefore, demand for the inferior product will fall. The reverse will happen when the income of the buyer falls.

If a direct relationship is established between income and demand, as shown in Figure-4.5, at a given price P_1 then we get a positively slopped curve for a normal good while a backward slopping curve in case of an inferior good.

These curves show that when the income of the consumer rises from Y_1 to Y_2, demand for a normal product will go up Figure(a) while that for an inferior product will go down once income exceeds OY_1 level Figure (b).

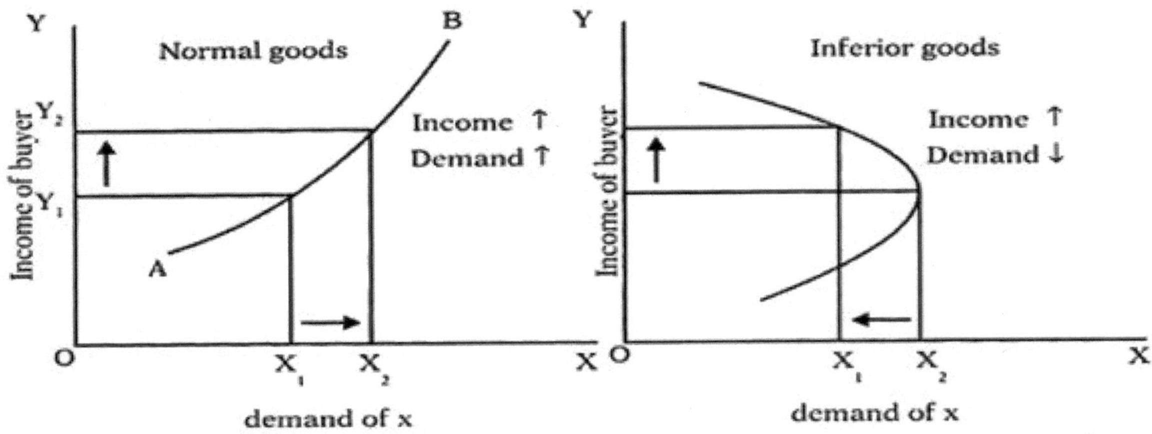

Fig(a): Normal Good Fig(b): Inferior Good

This is also called as income demand of a buyer expressed as, $Q_x = f(Y)$.

Determinant 6. The wealth of the Consumer (W):

Wealthy persons are characterized by high-income levels. Their propensity to consume is low and they save a larger proportion of their income. They spent a lesser proportion on consumables. The overall demand of a rich person is, thus, less vis-a-vis resources available at his disposal.

If the value of wealth erodes, say due to inflation in the economy, the rich person will save more to restore the total value of assets. As such, their demand will further fall. This adversely affects the total demand in an economy. Moreover, their total demand constitutes more luxury goods than necessities.

Determinant 7. Tastes, Preferences, and Fashion:

Tastes, preferences, and fashion also make a significant impact on demand. Generally speaking, if the tastes and preferences of a buyer move away from a product, its demand curve shifts downward and if the buyer prefers a particular product in terms of taste and preferences, its demand curve shifts upward Figure. For this, one can observe that demand for fashion goods is usually high.

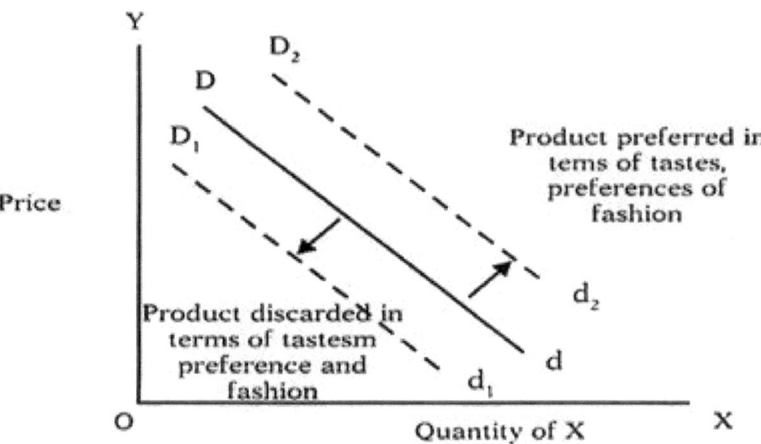

Fig: Demand curve shifts doward

However, no logical generalization can be made concerning this factor for being a subjective one. That is, a product may be preferred by a consumer while another consumer, at the same time, may dislike it.

For example, under the influence of western culture, demand for the traditional Indian male dress, Dhoti-kurta, has gone down considerably in urban areas while in rural areas, the majority of people still wear them. Demand for western food items, like burgers, pizzas and, pasta, are on the rise among the youth in metro cities while others still enjoy only traditional ethnic food.

For being subjective and qualitative, this determinant is often kept out in demand estimating or analyzing exercises. Incidentally, it is the only variable in the demand function that represents non-quantifiable subjective variables while other independent variables are quantifiable.

Determinant 8. Price Expectations:

If the price of the product is expected to rise in the future, for whatsoever reason, the consumer will demand more to stock the product and vice versa. In this way, he will save himself from future price hikes or extract benefits by postponing purchases in the anticipation of price fall. Thus, price expectations will also make a significant impact on the demand pattern of a buyer.

Determinant 9. Population:

The size of the population affects the market demand or demand at an aggregate level. Market demand for food grains and pulses, for example, will be more if the size population of a country is more. In short, the larger the population more will be the market demand and the smaller the population lesser will be the market demand.

Determinant 10. Size and Distribution of National Income:

Larger the size of the national income more will be the demand for goods and services. Further, an even distribution of national income will push the demand for necessities up while an uneven distribution will boost the demand for luxury goods.

Determinant 11. Availability of Credit:

Easy access to credit will push the demand up. People with smaller budgets will also able to purchase expensive products, consumer durables in particular, and pay in monthly installments afterward.

It will add new consumers leading the market demand to rise. Firms in the business of goods like LCD television sets, automatic washing machines, refrigerators, and luxury cars widely use this instrument for increasing their market demand and sales.

Determinant 12. Demonstration Effect:

The international demonstration effect of Ragnar Nurkse explains developing nations imitating the consumption patterns of developed nations. This is more clearly visible when a developing nation follows globalization policies aggressively.

Likewise, the middle-income population of a developing nation is often found imitating the rich in terms of lifestyle. All these, which are part of the demonstration effect, push demand, especially of luxury goods, up in the developing societies.

Determinant 13. Sale Promotion Strategies of Firms:

All firms in a market-driven economy introduce measures to increase their respective sales which include advertisement, appointing sales representatives, granting concession to buyers under different schemes, gifts, etc. All such measures encourage buyers to buy more, as also new buyers to buy the product. This affects the aggregate demand of a product to a significant extent.

Determinant 14. Taxation and Subsidies:

Government taxation also affects the demand for a product. A tax concession will lead the price of a product to fall and its demand to rise while the imposition of a new tax or increase in tax burden will lower the demand. Similarly, government subsidies also increase the demand for products. In short, lower taxes and higher subsidies will enhance the demand for a product and vice versa.

Determinant 15. Role of Different Determinants:

Apart from the variables discussed above, there may be many more determinants affecting the demand of a product though to a varying extent. Conceptually speaking, the demand function needs to be written separately concerning each product and for each buyer in which different variables will play a different role. To be precise, some factors may be important for one product but the same variables could be insignificant for others. Similarly, the importance of different variables may be different across buyers. Nonetheless, some generalizations can still be attempted.

THE LAW OF DEMAND

The law of demand describes the general tendency of a consumer's behavior in demanding a commodity about the changes in its price. It simply States that demand varies inversely to changes in price.

STATEMENT OF LAW OF DEMAND

Ceteris Paribus, the higher the price of a commodity, the smaller is the quantity demanded, and the lower the price, the larger the quantity demanded.

The conventional law of demand relates to the much-simplified demand function

$$D=f(p)$$

Where D represents demand, p the price, and f connotes a functional relationship.

ASSUMPTIONS OF LAW OF DEMAND

1. No change in consumer's income- If the level of a buyer's income changes he may buy more even at a higher price, invalidating the law of demand.
2. No change in consumer's preferences- The consumer's tastes, habits, and preferences should remain constant.
3. No change in the fashion- If the commodity concerned goes out of the fashion, a buyer may not buy more of it even at a substantial price of reduction.
4. No change in the price of related goods- Prices of other goods like substitutes and supportive,i.e, complementary or jointly demanded products remain unchanged.
5. No expectation of future price changes or shortages- The law requires that the given price change for the commodity is a normal one and has no speculative consideration.
6. No change in size, age composition, and sex ratio of the population – It is necessary that the number of buyers, their preferences, age structure, and sex ratio should remain constant, otherwise, there will be additional buyers in the market, so the total market demand may contract with a price rise.
7. No change in the range of goods available to the consumers- This implies that there is no innovation and arrival of new varieties of product in the market Which may distort consumer's preferences.
8. No change in the distribution of income and wealth of the commodity – There is no redistribution of incomes either so that the levels of income of the consumers remain the same.
9. No change in government policy- Changes in taxes may cause changes in consumer's income or commodity taxes and may lead to distortion in consumer's preferences.
10. No change in the weather conditions- It is assumed that the climate and weather conditions are unchanged in affecting the demand for certain goods like woolen clothes, umbrellas, etc.

EXPLANATION OF THE LAW OF DEMAND

Price of the commodity X (in Rs.)	Quantity demanded (units per week)
5	100
4	200
3	300
2	400
1	500

Fig: Demand Schedule

A Market demand schedule

The table represents a hypothetical demand schedule for commodity x. We can read from this table that with a fall in price at each stage demand tends to rise. There is an inverse relationship between price and quantity demanded.

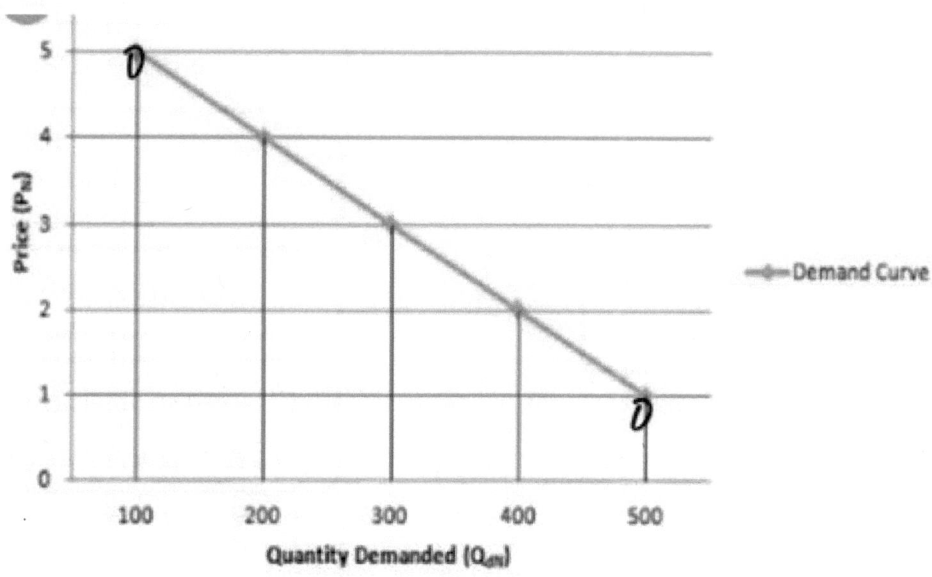

Fig: Curve Slopes down

In the above diagram, DD is a downward sloping demand curve indicating an inverse relationship between price and quantity demanded. From the given market demand curve one can easily locate the market demand for a product at a given price. Further, the demand curve geometrically represents the mathematical demand function: Dx=f(Px).

Exceptions to the Law of Demand

There are certain situations where the law of demand does not apply or becomes ineffective, i.e. with a fall in the price the demand falls, and with the price rise, the demand rises are called the **e**xceptions to the law of demand.

Exceptions to the Law of Demand

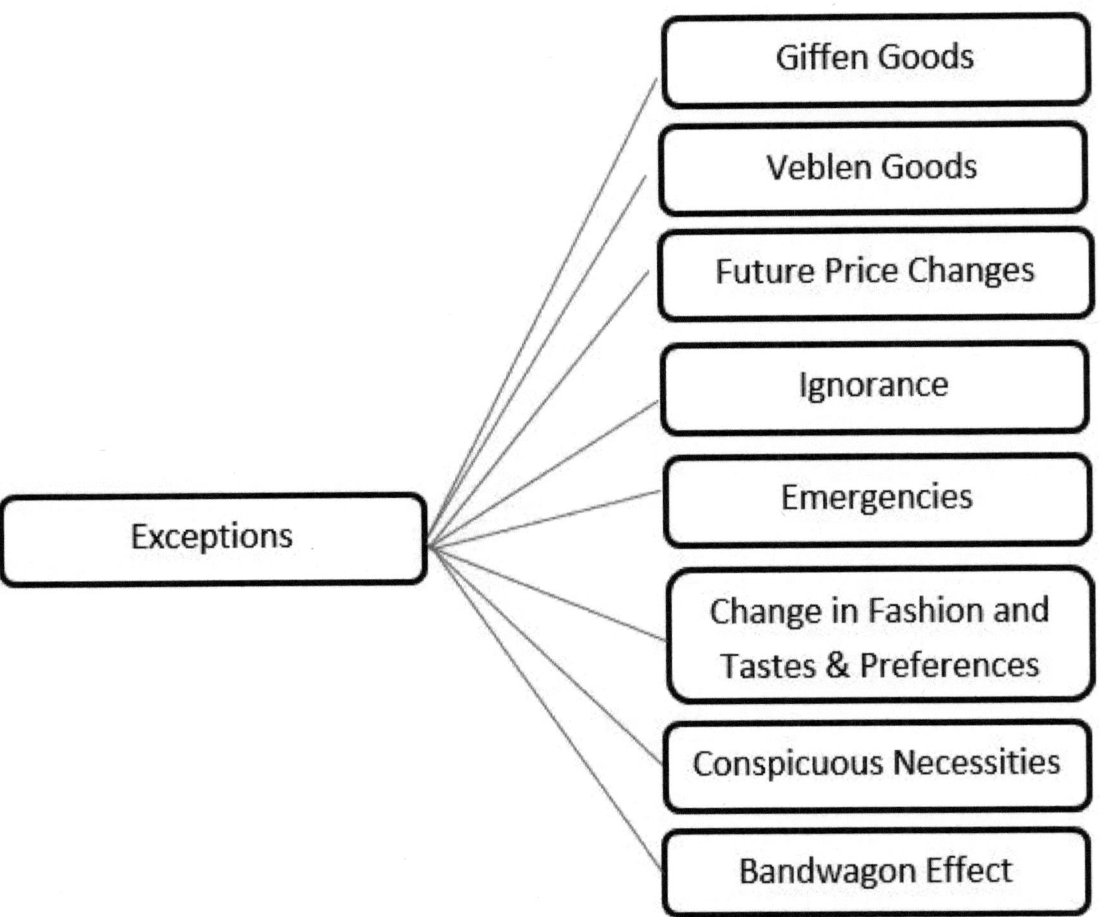

Fig: Exceptions to the Law of Demand

Giffen Goods: Giffen goods are inferior goods whose demand increases with the increase in their prices. There are several inferior commodities, much cheaper than the superior substitutes often consumed by the poor households as an essential commodity. Whenever the price of the Giffen goods increases its quantity demanded also increases because, with an increase in the price, and the income remains the same, the poor people cut the consumption of superior substitutes and buy more quantities of Giffen goods to meet their basic needs.

For Example, Suppose the minimum monthly consumption of food grains by a poor household is 20 Kg Bajra (Inferior good) and 10 Kg Rice (superior-good). The selling price of Bajra is Rs 5 per kg, and the rice is Rs 10 per kg, and the household spends its total income of Rs 200 on the purchase of these items. Suppose, the price of Bajra rose to Rs 6 per kg then the household will be forced to reduce the consumption of rice by 5 Kg and increase the quantity of Bajra to 25 Kg to meet the minimum monthly requirement of food grains of 30 kg.

Veblen Goods: Another exception to the law of demand is given by the economist Thorstein Veblen, who proposed the concept of **"Conspicuous Consumption."** According to Veblen, there are a certain group of people who measure the utility of the commodity purely by its price, which means, they think that higher-priced goods and services derive more utility than the lesser-priced commodities.

For example, goods like a diamond, platinum, ruby, etc. are bought by the upper echelons of the society (rich class) for whom the higher the price of these goods, the higher is the prestige value, and ultimately the higher is the utility or desirability of them.

The expectation of Price Change in the Future: When the consumer expects that the price of a commodity is likely to further increase in the future, then he will buy more of it despite its increased price to escape himself from the pinch of much higher price in the future.

On the other hand, if the consumer expects the price of the commodity to further fall in the future, then he will likely postpone his purchase despite less price of the commodity to avail the benefits of much lower prices in the future.

Ignorance: Often people are misconceived as high-priced commodities are better than low-priced commodities and rest their purchase decision on such a notion. They buy those commodities whose prices are relatively higher than the substitutes.

Emergencies: During emergencies such as war, natural calamity- flood, drought, earthquake, etc., the law of demand becomes ineffective. In such situations, people often fear the shortage of essentials and hence demand more goods and services even at higher prices.

Change in fashion and Tastes & Preferences: The change in fashion trends and tastes and preferences of consumers negates the effect of the law of demand. The consumer tends to buy those commodities which are very much 'in' in the market even at higher prices.

Conspicuous Necessities: Certain commodities have become essentials of modern life. These are the goods which consumer buys irrespective of an increase in the price. For example TV, refrigerator, automobiles, washing machines, air conditioners, etc.

Bandwagon Effect: This is the most common type of exception to the law of demand wherein the consumer tries to purchase those commodities which are bought by his friends, relatives, or neighbors. Here, the person tries to emulate the buying behavior and patterns of the group to which he belongs irrespective of the price of the commodity.

For example, if the majority of group members have smartphones then the consumer will also demand the smartphone even if the prices are high.

Thus, these are some of the exceptions to the law of demand where the demand curve is upward sloping, i.e. the demand increases with an increase in the price and decreases with the price decrease.

Changes in Demand and Quantity Demanded – (With Diagram)

In economics the terms change in quantity demanded and change in demand are two different concepts.

Change in quantity demanded refers to a change in the quantity purchased due to an increase or decrease in the price of a product. In such a case, it is incorrect to say increase or decrease in demand rather it is an increase or decrease in the quantity demanded.

On the other hand, change in demand refers to an increase or decrease in demand of a product due to various determinants of demand, while keeping the price constant.

Changes in quantity demanded can be measured by the movement of the demand curve, while changes in demand are measured by shifts in the demand curve. The term, change in quantity demanded refers to expansion or contraction of demand, while the change in demand means to increase or decrease in demand.

1. Expansion and Contraction of Demand:

The variations in the quantities demanded of a product with change in its price, while other factors are at constant, are termed as expansion or contraction of demand. Expansion of demand refers to the period when the quantity demanded is more because of the fall in the prices of a product. However, contraction of demand takes place when the quantity demanded is less due to a rise in the price o a product.

For example, consumers would reduce the consumption of milk in case the prices of milk increase and vice versa. Expansion and contraction are represented by the movement along the same demand curve. Movement from one point to another in a downward direction shows the expansion of demand, while an upward movement demonstrates the contraction of demand.

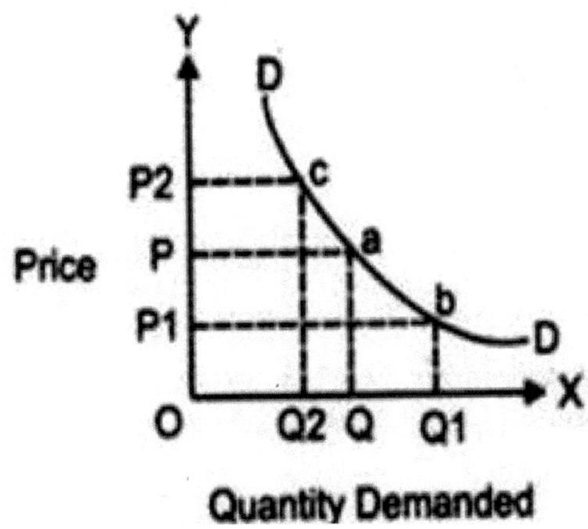

Figure-11 demonstrates the expansion and contraction of demand:

When the price changes from OP to OP1 and demand moves from OQ to OQ1, it shows the expansion of demand. However, the movement of price from OP to OP2 and movement of demand from OQ to OQ2 show the contraction of demand.

2. Increase and Decrease in Demand:

An increase and decrease in demand are referred to as a change in demand due to changes in various other factors such as a change in income, distribution of income, change in consumer's tastes and preferences, change in the price of related goods, while Price factor is kept constant Increase in demand refers to the rise in demand of a product at a given price.

On the other hand, a decrease in demand refers to the fall in demand for a product at a given price. For example, essential goods, such as salt would be consumed in equal quantity, irrespective of increase or decrease in its price. Therefore, an increase in demand implies that there is an increase in demand for a product at any price. Similarly, a decrease in demand can also be referred to as the same quantity demanded at a lower price, as the quantity demanded at a higher price.

The increase and decrease in demand are represented as the shift in the demand curve. In the graphical representation of the demand curve, the shifting of demand is demonstrated as the movement from one demand curve to another demand curve. In case of an increase in demand, the demand curve shifts to right, while in the case of a decrease in demand, it shifts to the left of the original demand curve.

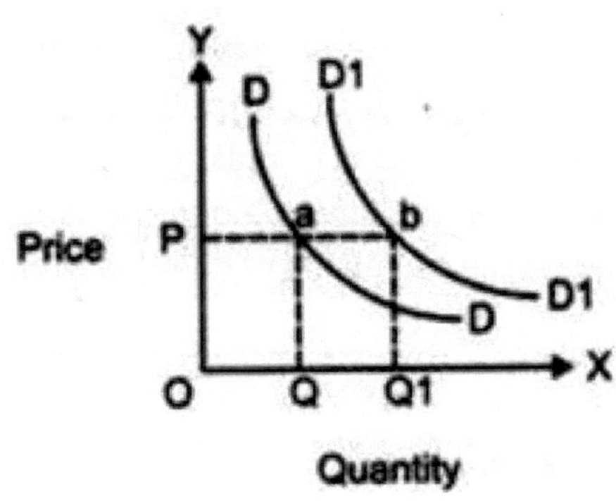

Figure-12 shows the increase and decrease in demand

In Figure-12, the movement from DD to D1D1 shows the increase in demand with price at constant (OP). However, the quantity has also increased from OQ to OQ1.

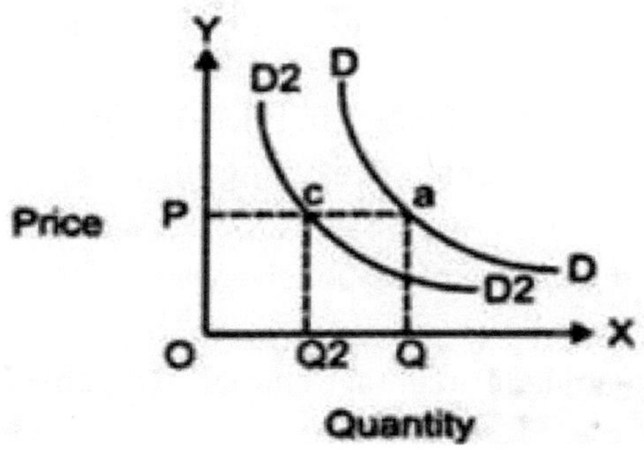

Figure-13 shows the decrease in demand

In Figure-13, the movement from DD to D2D2 shows the decrease in demand with price at constant (OP). However, the quantity has also decreased from OQ to OQ2.

Elasticity of Demand

A change in the price of a commodity affects its demand. We can find the elasticity of demand, or the degree of responsiveness of demand by comparing the percentage price changes with the quantities demanded. In this article, we will look at the concept of elasticity of demand and take a quick look at its various types.

Elasticity of Demand

To begin with, let's look at the definition of the elasticity of demand: "Elasticity of demand is the responsiveness of the quantity demanded of a commodity to changes in one of the variables on which demand depends. In other words, it is the percentage change in quantity demanded divided by the percentage in one of the variables on which demand depends."

The variables on which demand can depend are:

- Price of the commodity
- Prices of related commodities
- Consumer's income, etc.

Let's look at some examples:

a. The price of a radio falls from Rs. 500 to Rs. 400 per unit. As a result, the demand increases from 100 to 150 units.
b. Due to government subsidy, the price of wheat falls from Rs. 10/kg to Rs. 9/kg. Due to this, the demand increases from 500 kilograms to 520 kilograms.

In both cases above, you can notice that as the price decreases, the demand increases. Hence, the demand for radios and wheat responds to price changes.

Types of Elasticity of Demand

Based on the variable that affects the demand, the elasticity of demand is of the following types. One point to note is that unless otherwise mentioned, whenever the elasticity of demand is mentioned, it implies price elasticity.

Price Elasticity

The price elasticity of demand is the response of the quantity demanded to change the price of a commodity. It is assumed that the consumer's income, tastes, and prices of all other goods are steady. It is measured as a percentage change in the quantity demanded divided by the percentage change in price. Therefore,

Price Elasticity=Ep= Percentage change in quantity demanded Percentage change in price

Or,

Ep = Change in Quantity×100Original Quantity Change in Price×100Original Price

=Change in Quantity Original Quantity × Original Price Change in Price

Income Elasticity

The income elasticity of demand is the degree of responsiveness of the quantity demanded to a change in the consumer's income. Symbolically,

EI=Percentage change in quantity demanded Percentage change in income

Cross Elasticity

The cross elasticity of demand of a commodity X for another commodity Y, is the change in demand of commodity X due to a change in the price of commodity Y. Symbolically,

Ec=ΔqxΔpy×pyqx

Where,

Ec is the cross elasticity,

Δqx is the original demand of commodity X,

Δqx is the change in demand of X,

Δpy is the original price of commodity Y, and

Δpy is the change in the price of Y.

Degrees of Price Elasticity of Demand

Dr. Marshall has pro-founded the concept of price elasticity of demand. In simple words, price elasticity of demand is the ratio of percentage change in quantity demanded to the percentage change in price.

In other words, price elasticity of demand is a measure of the relative change in quantity purchased of a good in response to a relative change in its price. It is thus, the rate at which the demand changes to the given change in prices.

So, we can say that it is the rate or the degree of response in demand to the change in price.

Therefore, the co-efficient of price elasticity of demand can be written as below:

$$Ed = \frac{\text{Proportionate change in Demand}}{\text{Proportionate change in Price}}$$

Symbolically :

$$Ed = \frac{\Delta q}{q} / \frac{\Delta p}{p} = \frac{\Delta q}{q} \div \frac{\Delta p}{p}$$

$$Ed = \frac{\Delta q}{q} \times \frac{p}{\Delta p} = \frac{\Delta q}{\Delta p} \times \frac{p}{q}$$

Definitions:

The concept of price elasticity of demand has been defined by different economies as under:

"Elasticity of demand may be defined as the percentage change in quantity demanded to the percentage change in price."

"Elasticity of demand is the ratio of relative change in quantity to the relative change in price."

" The elasticity of demand for a commodity is the rate at which quantity bought to change the price change."

"The elasticity of demand is a measure of the relative change in quantity to a relative change in price".

"Elasticity of demand measures the responsiveness of demand to changes in price".

Degrees of Price Elasticity:

Different commodities have different price elasticities. Some commodities have more elastic demand while others have relatively elastic demand. The price elasticity of demand ranges from zero to infinity. It can be equal to zero, less than one, greater than one, and equal to unity.

"The elasticity or responsiveness of demand in a market is great or small according to as the amount demanded increases much or little for a given fall in price and diminishes much or little for a given rise in price".

However, some particular values of elasticity of demand have been explained as under:

1. Perfectly Elastic Demand:

Perfectly elastic demand is said to happen when a little change in price leads to an infinite change in quantity demanded. A small rise in price on the part of the seller reduces the demand to zero. In such a case the shape of the demand curve will be a horizontal straight line as shown in figure1.

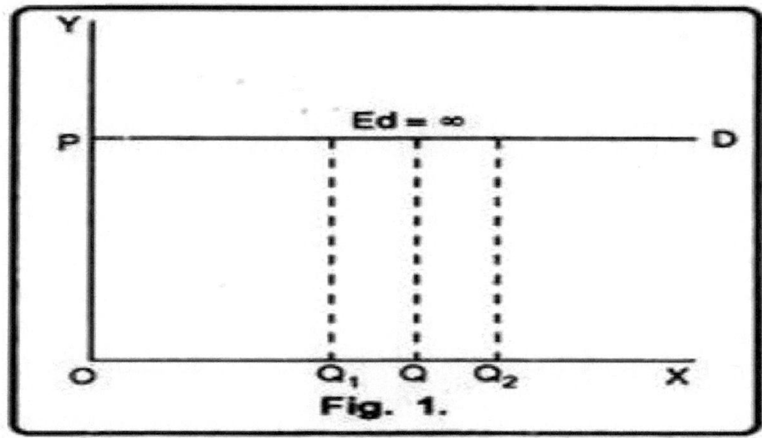

Figure representing the perfectly elastic demand

Figure1 shows that at the ruling price OP, the demand is infinite. A slight price rise will contract the demand to zero. A slight fall in price will attract more consumers but the elasticity of demand will remain infinite ($e_d=\infty$). But in the real world, the cases of perfectly elastic demand are exceedingly rare and are not of any practical interest.

2. Perfectly Inelastic Demand:

Perfectly inelastic demand is opposite to perfectly elastic demand. Under the perfectly inelastic demand, irrespective of any rise or fall in the price of a commodity, the quantity demanded remains the same. The elasticity of demand in this case will be equal to zero ($e_d = 0$).

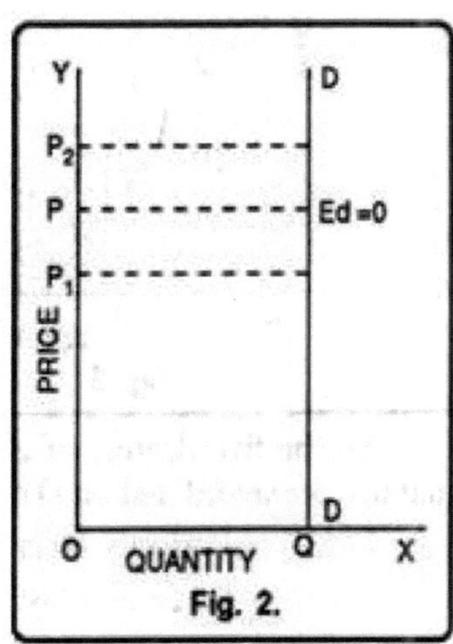

Figure representing perfectly inelastic demand

In figure2 DD shows the perfectly inelastic demand. At price OP, the quantity demanded is OQ. Now, the price falls to OP_1, from OP, the demand remains the same. Similarly, if the price rises to OP_2 the demand remains the same. But just as we do not see the example of perfectly elastic demand in the real world, in the same fashion, it is difficult to come across the cases of perfectly inelastic demand because even the demand for, bare essentials of life does show some degree of responsiveness to change in price.

3. Unitary Elastic Demand:

The demand is said to be unitary elastic when a given proportionate change in the price level brings about an equal proportionate change in quantity demanded. The numerical value of unitary elastic demand is exactly one i.e. Marshall calls it unit elastic.

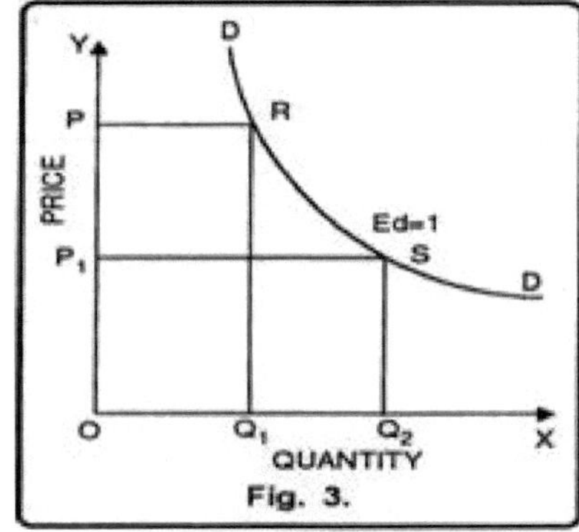

Fig. 3.

Figure reprenting Unitary Elastic Demand

In figure 3, DD demand curve represents unitary elastic demand. This demand curve is called a rectangular hyperbola. When the price is OP, the quantity demanded is OQ\. Now price falls to OP_1 the quantity demanded increases to OQ2. The area OQ\RP = area OP\SQ$_2$ in the fig. denotes that in all cases price elasticity of demand is equal to one.

4. Relatively Elastic Demand:

Relatively elastic demand refers to a situation in which a small change in price leads to a big change in quantity demanded. In such a case elasticity of demand is said to be more than one ($e_d > 1$). This has been shown in figure 4.

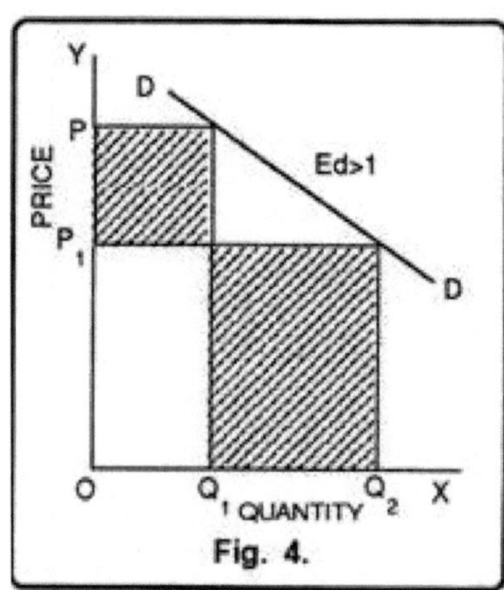

Fig. 4.

Figure representing Relatively Elastic Demand

In fig. 4, DD is the demand curve which indicates that when the price is OP the quantity demanded is OQ_1. Now the price falls from OP to OP_1, the quantity demanded increases from OQ_1 to OQ_2 i.e. quantity demanded changes more than the price change.'

5. Relatively Inelastic Demand:

Under the relatively inelastic demand, a given percentage change in price produces a relatively less percentage change in quantity demanded. In such a case elasticity of demand is said to be less than one ($e_d < 1$). It has been shown in figure 5.

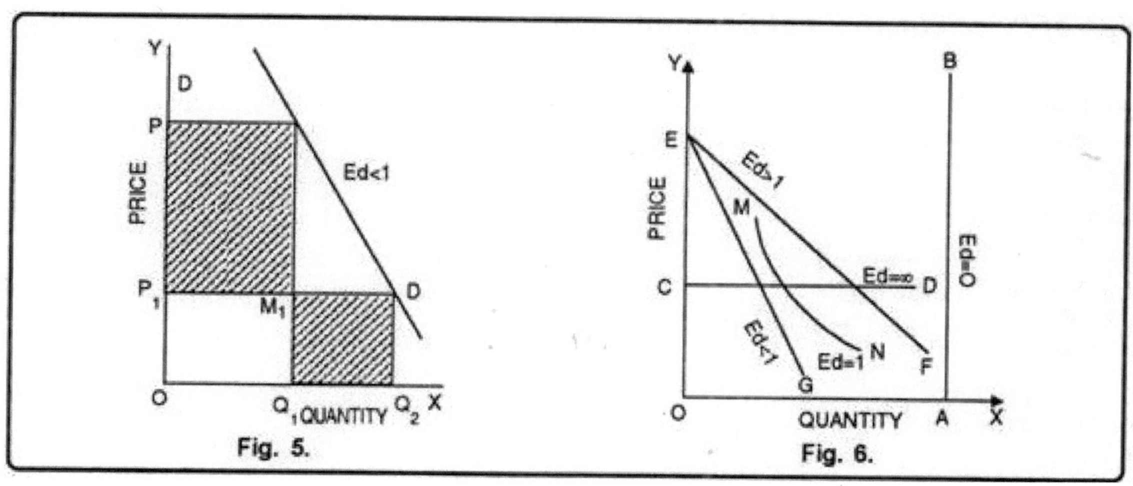

Figure representing Relatively Inelastic Demand

All the five degrees of elasticity of demand have been shown in figure 6. On OX axis, quantity demanded, and on OY axis price is given.

It shows:

1. AB — Perfectly Inelastic Demand
2. CD — Perfectly Elastic Demand

3. EG — Less than Unitary Elastic Demand
4. EF — Greater Than Unitary Elastic Demand
5. MN — Unitary Elastic Demand.

Mathematical Expression of Price Elasticity of Demand

The price elasticity of demand is defined as the percentage change in quantity demanded due to a certain percentage change in price.

Mathematically, it can be expressed as:

$$\text{Price elasticity of demand} = \frac{\%\text{change in quantity demanded}}{\%\text{change in price}}$$

Symbolically, it can be expressed as:

$$E_p = \frac{\Delta q}{\Delta p} \times \frac{p}{q}$$

Where E_p= Price elasticity of demand
q= Original quantity demanded
Δq = Change in quantity demanded
p= Original price
Δp = Change in price

Calculation of Price Elasticity of Demand

Suppose that price of a commodity falls from Rs.10 to Rs.9 per unit and due to this, the quantity demanded of the commodity increased from 100 units to 120 units. What is the price elasticity of demand?

Give that,
p= initial price= Rs.10
q= initial quantity demanded= 100 units
Δp=change in price=Rs. (10-9) = Rs.1
Δq=change in quantity demanded= (120-100) units = 20 units
Now,

$$\therefore E_p = \frac{\Delta q}{\Delta p} \times \frac{p}{q}$$
$$= \frac{20}{1} \times \frac{10}{100}$$
$$= \frac{2}{1}$$
$$= 2\%$$

The quantity demanded increases by 2% due to a fall in price by Rs.1.

Factors affecting price elasticity of demand

The number of close substitutes – the more close substitutes there are in the market, the more elastic is demand because consumers find it easy to switch. E.g. Air travel and train travel are weak substitutes for inter-continental flights but closer substitutes for journeys of around 200-400km e.g. between major cities in a large country.

The cost of switching between products – there may be costs involved in switching. In this case, demand tends to be inelastic. For example, mobile phone service providers may insist on a12 monthly contract which has the effect of locking in some consumers once a choice has been made

The degree of necessity or whether the good is a luxury – necessities tend to have an inelastic demand whereas luxuries tend to have a more elastic demand. An example of a necessity is rare-earth metals which are an essential raw material in the manufacture of solar cells, batteries. China produces 97% of the total output of rare-earth metals – giving them monopoly power in this market

The proportion of a consumer's income allocated to spending on the good – products that take up a high % of income will have a more elastic demand

The period allowed following a price change – demand is more price elastic, the longer that consumers have to respond to a price change. They have more time to search for cheaper substitutes and switch their spending.

Whether the good is subject to habitual consumption – consumers become less sensitive to the price of the good if they buy something out of habit (it has become the default choice).

Peak and off-peak demand - demand is price inelastic at peak times and more elastic at off-peak times – this is particularly the case for transport services.

The breadth of the definition of a good or service – if a good is broadly defined, i.e. the demand for petrol or meat, demand is often inelastic. But specific brands of petrol or beef are likely to be more elastic following a price change.

Price Elasticity of Demand (Practical Applications)

The following points highlight the nine main practical applications of the concept of price elasticity of demand. The uses are:

Practical Application 1. Effects of Changes in Price Upon Demand:

The concept is very useful to study the reactions of the demand for a commodity to the changes in its price. If the demand is elastic, a small change in the price brings about a considerable change in the quantity demanded, but in the case of inelastic demand, this consequential change in demand is relatively small.

Practical Application 2. Effects of Changes in Price on Revenue:

The concept enables us to determine the condition of equilibrium of a firm. And a profit-maximizing firm reaches equilibrium when revenue = marginal cost.

Practical Application 3. Monopoly Pricing:

The concept is useful in monopoly price- decisions. The monopolist, being the sole supplier of a particular commodity, can raise the price but cannot affect the demand pattern of consumers. So, in fixing the price the monopolist will have, of necessity, to take note of the elasticity of demand for his product. He will fix the price at a low level when the demand is elastic and at a high level when it is inelastic.

Practical Application 4. Price Discrimination:

In perfect competition, the same price is charged from all the buyers. But, the downward slope of the demand curve of the monopolist gives scope for price discrimination. Price discrimination refers to the practice of charging different prices for the same product from different buyers at the same time. It can be profitably practiced only when the price elasticity of demand differs from market to market or from one segment of the market to another.

Practical Application 5. Wage Bargaining by Trade Unions:

The bargaining power of the trade unions in raising the wages of a group of labor in a particular industry also depends, among other things, on the elasticity of demand for their services to the employer. A trade union usually succeeds in raising wages when the demand for the services of labor to the employer is inelastic: because in such a case the employer cannot easily dispense with their services. On the other hand, it may not succeed when demand for labor is elastic.

Practical Application 6. Importance in Taxation:

Furthermore, the concept is a useful tool in taxation. A finance minister is to consider the elasticity of demand of the different commodities for taxation. If he pushes commodity tax (excise duty) rates up too much the consequent price increase may make the total tax yield even lower than before. On the other hand, a small tax reduction may increase the tax yield.

Practical Application 7. Importance in Determining the Incidence of Taxation:

The concept of the elasticity of demand, along with that of supply, is used to determine the shifting and incidence of a tax. When a tax is imposed on a commodity of inelastic demand, the seller can generally transfer the burden of the tax upon the consumers by raising the price, and so the incidence of the tax falls upon the buyers.

Practical Application 8. Price Determination of Joint-cost Products:

Again, in the case of the joint-cost products (e.g., cotton fiber and cotton seeds) where the cost of each cannot be separately determined, the criterion of demand elasticity is applied in determining their prices.

Practical Application 9. Economic Policy:

The knowledge of elasticity is also valuable in the formation of economic policies, too. This point may now be illustrated. A country suffering from balance of payments problems may try to tackle the imbalance by devaluing its currency.

Measuring Price Elasticity of Demand:

The following points highlight the top four methods used for measuring the elasticity of demand. The methods are:-

1. The Percentage Method
2. The Point Method
3. The Arc Method
4. Total Outlay Method.

1. The Percentage Method:

The price elasticity of demand is measured by its coefficient (E_p). This coefficient (E_p) measures the percentage change in the quantity of a commodity demanded resulting from a given percentage change in its price.

Thus

$$E_p = \frac{\%\ change\ in\ q}{\%\ change\ in\ p} = \frac{\Delta q / q}{\Delta p / p} = \frac{\Delta q}{\Delta p} \times \frac{p}{q}$$

Where q refers to quantity demanded, p to price, and Δ to change. If $E_P > 1$, demand is elastic. If $E_P < 1$, demand is inelastic, and $E_p = 1$, demand is unitary elastic.

With this formula, we can compute price elasticities of demand based on a demanding schedule.

Table.1 : Demand Schedule

Combination	*Price (Rs.) Per Kg. of X*	*Quantity Kgs.of X*
A	6	0
B	5	10
C	4	20
D	3	30
E	2	40
F	1	50
G	0	60

Table represent Demand Schedule

Let us first take combinations B and D.

(i) Suppose the price of commodity X falls from Rs. 5 per kg. to Rs. 3 per kg. and its quantity demanded increases from 10 kgs. to 30 kgs.

Then

$$E_p = \frac{\Delta q}{\Delta p} \times \frac{p}{q} = \frac{(30-10)}{(3-5)} \times \frac{5}{10} = \frac{20}{-2} \times \frac{5}{10} = -5 \text{ or } > 1.$$

This shows elastic demand or elasticity of demand greater than unitary.

Note:

The formula can be understood like this:

$\Delta q = q_2 - q_2$ where q_2 is the new quantity (30 kgs.) and q_i the original quantity (10 kgs.).

$\Delta P = p_2 - p_1$ where p_2 is the new price (Rs.3) and p_l the original price (Rs. 5).

In the formula, p refers to the original price (p_1) and q to the original quantity (q_1). The opposite is the example case (i) below, where Rs. 3 becomes the original price and 30 kgs. as the original quantity.

(ii) Let us measure elasticity by moving in the reverse direction. Suppose the price of Arises from Rs. 3 per kg. to Rs. 5 per kg. and the quantity demanded decreases from 30 kgs. to 10 kgs.

Then

$$E_p = \frac{\Delta q}{\Delta p} \times \frac{p}{q} = \frac{(10-30)}{(5-3)} \times \frac{3}{30} = \frac{-20}{2} \times \frac{3}{30} = -1$$

This shows the unitary elasticity of demand.

Notice that the value of Ep in example (ii) differs from that in example (i) depending on the direction in which we move. This difference in the elasticities is due to the use of a different base in computing percentage changes in each case.

Now consider combinations D and F.

(iii) Suppose the price of commodity X falls from Rs. 3 per kg to Re.lper kg. and its quantity demanded increases from 30 kgs. to 50 kgs.

Then

$$E_p = \frac{\Delta q}{\Delta p} \times \frac{p}{q} = \frac{(50-30)}{(1-3)} \times \frac{3}{30} = \frac{20}{2} \times \frac{3}{30} = -1$$

This is again unitary elasticity.

(iv) Take the reverse order when the price rises from Re. 1 per kg. to Rs. 3 per kg. and the quantity demanded decreases from 50 kgs. to 30 kgs.

Then

$$E_p = \frac{\Delta q}{\Delta p} \times \frac{p}{q} = \frac{(30-50)}{3-1} \times \frac{1}{50} = \frac{-20}{2} \times \frac{1}{50} = -\frac{1}{5} < 1$$

This shows inelastic demand or less than unitary.

The value of E_p again differs in this example than that given in example (iii) for the reason stated above.

2. The Point Method:

Prof. Marshall devised a geometrical method for measuring elasticity at a point on the demand curve. Let RS be a straight-line demand curve in Figure. 2. If the price falls from PB (= OA) to MD (= OC), the quantity demanded increases from OB to OD.

Elasticity at point P on the RS demand curve according to the formula is:

EP = Δq/Δp x p/q

Where Δq represents the change in quantity demanded, Δp changes in price level while p and q are initial prices and quantity levels.

$\Delta q = BD = QM$

$\Delta p = PQ$

$p = PB$

$q = OB$

Substituting these values in the elasticity formula:

$$E_p = \frac{QM}{PQ} \times \frac{PB}{OB}$$

Moreover, $\frac{QM}{PQ} \times \frac{BS}{PB}$

[$\angle PQM = \angle PBS$ being right angles and PQM and PBS are similar Δ_s]

$$\therefore \frac{BS}{PB} \times \frac{PB}{OB} = \frac{BS}{OB}$$

Since, ΔPBS and ΔROS are similar,

$$Ep \text{ at point } P = \frac{BS}{OB} = \frac{OA}{AR} = \frac{PS}{PR} = \frac{\textit{Lower Segment}}{\textit{Upper Segment}}$$

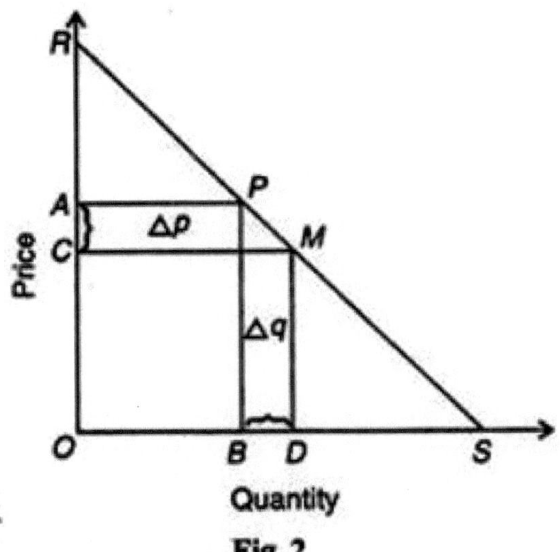

Fig. 2

With the help of the point method, it is easy to point out elasticity at any point along a demand curve. Suppose that the straight-line demand curve DC in Figure. 3 is 6 centimeters. Five points L, M, N, P, and Q are taken on this demand curve. The elasticity of demand at each point can be known with the help of the above method. Let point N be in the middle of the demand curve. So elasticity of demand at the point

$$N = \frac{CN\ (Lower\ Segment)}{ND\ (Upper\ Segment)} = \frac{3}{3} = 1\ (Unity)$$

Elasticity of demand at point

$$M = \frac{CM}{MD} = \frac{5}{1} = 5 \text{ or } > 1.$$

(Greater than Unity)

Elasticity of demand at point

$$L = \frac{CL}{LD} = \frac{6}{0} = \infty\ (infinity).$$

Elasticity of demand at Point

$$P = \frac{CP}{PD} = \frac{1}{5} = (Less\ than\ Unity).$$

Elasticity of demand at point

$$Q = \frac{CQ}{QD} = \frac{0}{6} = 0\ (Zero)$$

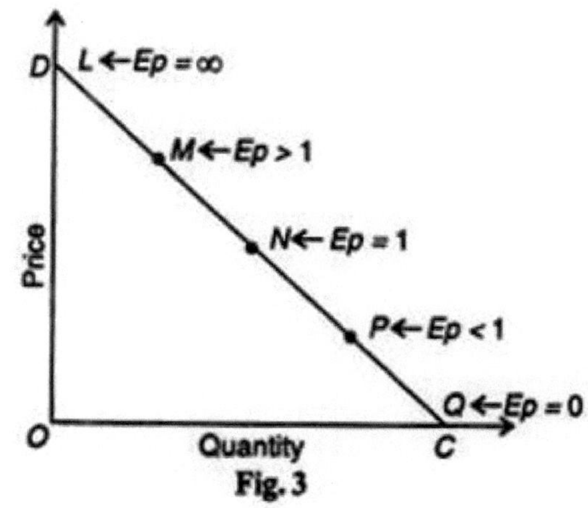

Fig. 3

We conclude that at the mid-point of the demand curve, the elasticity of demand is unity. Moving up the demand curve from the mid-point, elasticity becomes greater. When the demand curve touches the Y-axis, elasticity is infinity. Ipso facto, any point below the mid-point towards the A'-axis will show elastic demand. Elasticity becomes zero when the demand curve touches the X-axis.

3. The Arc Method:

We have studied the measurement of elasticity at a point on a demand curve. But when elasticity is measured between two points on the same demand curve, it is known as arc elasticity. In the words of Prof. Baumol, **"Arc elasticity is a measure of the average responsiveness to price change exhibited by a demand curve over some finite stretch of the curve."**

Any two points on a demand curve make an arc. The area between P and M on the DD curve in Figure. 4 is an arc that measures elasticity over a certain range of price and quantities. On any two points of a demand curve, the elasticity coefficients are likely to be different depending upon the method of computation. Consider the price-quantity combinations P and Mas given in Table..

Table 2: Demand Schedule

Point	*Price (Rs)*	*Quantity (Kg)*
P	8	10
M	6	12

table represent demand schedule

If we move in the reverse direction from M to P, then

$$\frac{(10-20)}{(8-6)} \times \frac{6}{12} = \frac{-2}{2} \times \frac{6}{12} = -\frac{1}{2}$$

Thus the point method of measuring elasticity at two points on a demand curve gives different elasticity coefficients because we used a different base in computing the percentage change in each case.

To avoid this discrepancy, elasticity for the arc (PM in Figure) is calculated by taking the average of the two prices $[(p_1 + p_2)^{½}]$ and the average of the two quantities $[(q_1 + q_2)^{½}]$. The formula for price elasticity of demand at the mid-point (C in Figure) of the arc on the demand curve is

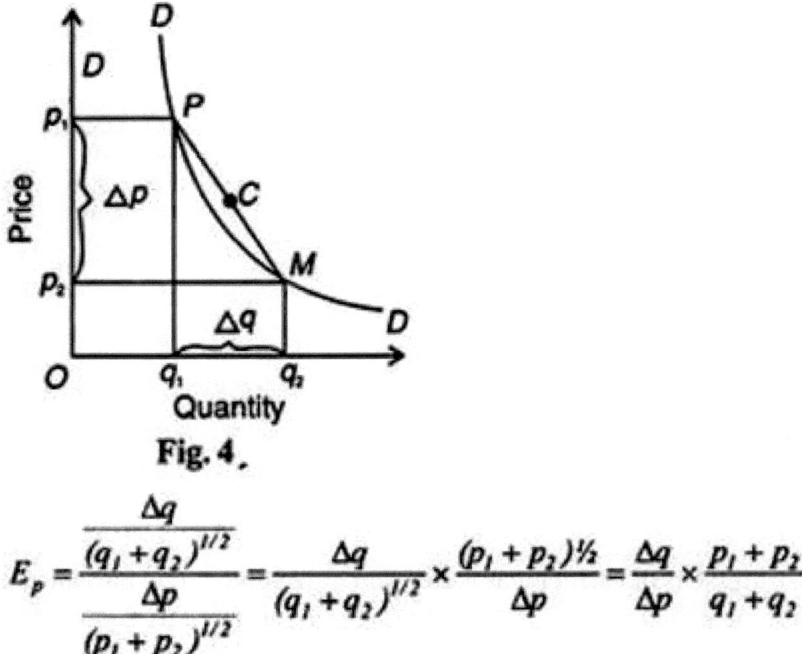

Fig. 4.

$$E_p = \frac{\dfrac{\Delta q}{(q_1+q_2)^{1/2}}}{\dfrac{\Delta p}{(p_1+p_2)^{1/2}}} = \frac{\Delta q}{(q_1+q_2)^{1/2}} \times \frac{(p_1+p_2)½}{\Delta p} = \frac{\Delta q}{\Delta p} \times \frac{p_1+p_2}{q_1+q_2}$$

Based on this formula, we can measure arc elasticity of demand when there is a movement either from point P to M or from M to P.

From P to M at point P, $p_1 = 8$, $q_1 = 10$, and at point M, $p_2 = 6$, $q_2 = 12$.

Applying these values, we get

$$E_p = \frac{\Delta q}{\Delta p} \times \frac{p_1+p_2}{q_1+q_2} = \frac{(12-10)}{6-8} \times \frac{(8+6)}{(10+12)} = \frac{2}{-2} \times \frac{14}{22} = -\frac{7}{11}$$

From *M* to *P* at point *M*, $P_1 = 6$, $q_1 = 12$ and at point, $p_2 = 8$, $q_2 = 10$.

Now we have $E_p = \dfrac{(10-12)}{(8-6)} \times \dfrac{(6+8)}{(12+10)} = \dfrac{-2}{2} \times \dfrac{14}{22} = -\dfrac{7}{11}$

Thus whether we move from M to P or P to M on the arc PM of the DD curve, the formula for arc elasticity of demand gives the same numerical value. The closer the two points P and M are, the more accurate is the measure of elasticity based on this formula.

If the two points which form the arc on the demand curve are so close that they almost merge into each other, the numerical value of arc elasticity equals the numerical value of point elasticity.

4. The Total Outlay Method:

Marshall evolved the total outlay, or total revenue, or total expenditure method as a measure of elasticity. By comparing the total expenditure of a purchaser both before and after the price change, it can be known whether his demand for a good is elastic, unity, or less elastic.

Total outlay is price multiplied by the quantity of a good purchased: Total Outlay = Price x Quantity Demanded. This is explained with the help of the demand schedule in Table.

Table. 3 : Total Outlay Method

Price Rs. per Kg.	*Quantity in Kgs.*	*TE in Rs*	*Ep*
(1)	(2)	(1×2)=3	(4)
9	2	18	
8	3	24	> 1
7	4	28	
6	5	30	
5	6	30	= 1
4	7.5	30	
3	8	24	
2	9	18	< 1
1	10	10	

table represents total outlay method

(i) Elastic Demand:

Demand is elastic, when with the fall in price the total expenditure increases, and with the rise in price the total expenditure decreases. Table.3 shows that when the price falls from Rs. 9 to Rs. 8, the total expenditure increases from Rs. 18 to Rs. 24, and when the price rises from Rs. 7 to Rs. 8, the total expenditure falls from Rs. 28 to Rs. 24. Demand is elastic(Ep > 1) in this case.

(ii) Unitary Elastic Demand:

When with the fall or rise in price, the total expenditure remains unchanged, the elasticity of demand is unity. This is shown in the table when with the fall in price from Rs. 6 to Rs. 5 or with the rise in price from Rs. 4 to Rs. 5, the total expenditure remains unchanged at Rs. 30, i.e., Ep=1

(iii) Less Elastic Demand:

Demand is less elastic if, with the fall in price, the total expenditure falls, and with the rise in price the total expenditure rises. In Table 3 when the price falls from Rs. 3 to Rs. 2, total expenditure falls from Rs. 24 to Rs 18, and when the price rises from Re. 1 to Rs. 2. the total expenditure also rises from Rs. 10 to Rs. 18. This is the case of inelastic or less elastic demand, Ep < 1.

Table summarises these relationships:

Total 4 : Total Outlay Method

Price	*TE*	*Ep*
Falls	Rises }	>1
Rises	Falls }	
Falls	Unchanged }	=1
Rises	Unchanged }	
Falls	Falls }	
Rises	Rises }	<1

Table represents total outlay method

The measurement of elasticity of demand in terms of the total outlay method is explained in Fig. where we divide the relationship between price elasticity of demand and total expenditure into three stages.

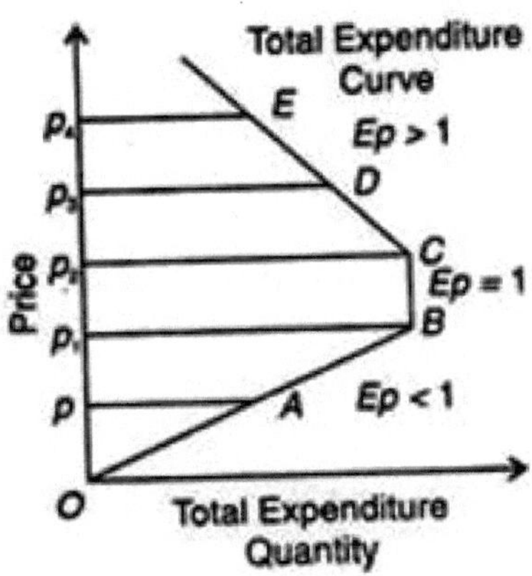

Fig: total layout method

In the first stage, when the price falls from OP_4 to OP_3 and OP_2respectively, the total expenditure rises from P_4 E to P_3 D and P_2 C respectively. On the other hand, when the price increases from OP_2 to OP_3 and OP_4, the total expenditure decreases from P_2 C to P_3 D and P_4E respectively.

Thus EC segment of the total expenditure curve shows elastic demand (Ep > 1).

In the second stage, when the price falls from OP_2 to OP_1 or rises from OP_1 to OP_2, the total expenditure equals, $P_2C = P_1B$, and the elasticity of demand is equal to the unity (Ep = 1).

In the third stage, when the price falls from Op_1 to Op, the total expenditure also falls from P_1 B to PA. Thus with the rise in price from OP to Op_1, the total expenditure also increases from PA to P_1B and the elasticity of demand is less than unity (Ep < 1).

Income Elasticity of Demand: Measurement, Types, and Significance

Consumer income is one of the important determinants of demand for a product.The demand for a product and consumer's income is directly related to each other, unlike the price-demand relationship.

"Income elasticity of demand means the ratio of the percentage change in the quantity demanded to the percentage in income"-Watson.

For example, the demand for a product increases with an increase in consumer s income and vice versa, while keeping other factors of demand constant. The degree of responsiveness of demand concerning change in consumer s income is called income elasticity of demand. According to Watson, "Income elasticity of demand means the ratio of the percentage change in the quantity demanded to the percentage in income."

Measurement of Income Elasticity of Demand:

The income elasticity of demand (e_y) can be measured by the following formula:

e_y = Percentage change in quantity demanded/Percentage change in income

Percentage change in quantity demanded = New quantity demanded (ΔQ)/Original quantity demanded (Q)

Percentage change in income = New income (ΔY)/original income (Y)

Therefore, the income elasticity of demand can be symbolically represented as:

$e_y = \Delta Q/Q : \Delta Y/Y$

$e_y = \Delta Q/Q * Y/\Delta Y$

$e_y = \Delta Q/\Delta Y * Y/Q$

Change in demand (ΔQ) is the difference between the new demand (Q1) and the original demand (Q).

It can be calculated by the following formula:

$\Delta Q = Q1 - Q$

Similarly, change in income is the difference between the new income (Y1) and original income (Y).

It can be calculated by the following formula:

$\Delta Y = Y1 - Y$

The formula for measuring the income elasticity of demand is same as price elasticity of demand. The only difference in the formula is that in the income elasticity of demand, income (Y) is substituted as a determinant of demand in place of price (P). Let us understand the concept of income elasticity of demand with the help of an example.

Suppose the monthly income of an individual increases from Rs. 6,000 (Y) to Rs. 12,000 (Y1). Now, his demand for clothes increases from 30 units (Q) to 60 units (Q1).

The income elasticity of demand can be calculated as follows:

$e_y = \Delta Q/\Delta Y * Y/Q$

$\Delta Q = Q1 - Q = 60 - 30 = 30$ units

$\Delta Y = Y1 - Y = 12000 - 6000 =$ Rs. 6000

$e_y = 30/6000 * 6000/30 = 1$ (equal to unity)

Types of Income Elasticity of Demand:

Like price elasticity of demand, the degree of responsiveness of demand with change in consumer's income is not always the same. The income elasticity of demand is different for different products.

Based on numerical value, income elasticity of demand is classified into three groups, which are as follows:

i. Positive Income Elasticity of Demand:

This refers to a situation when the demand for a product increases with an increase in consumer's income and decreases with a decrease in consumer's income. The income elasticity of demand is positive for normal goods.

It is explained with the help of Figure:

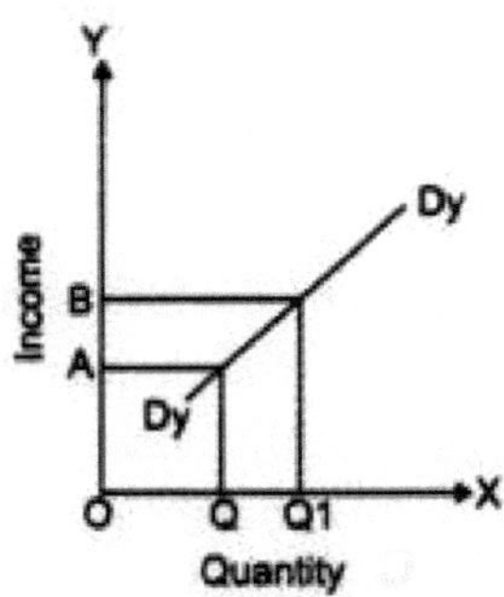

Fig: Positive elasticity of demand

In Figure, the slope of the curve is upward from left to right, which indicates that the increase in income causes an increase in demand and vice versa. Therefore, in such a case, the elasticity of demand is positive.

The positive income elasticity of demand can be of three types, which are discussed as follows:

a. Unitary Income Elasticity of Demand:

This implies that positive income elasticity of demand would be unitary when the proportionate change in the quantity demanded is equal to the proportionate change in income. For example, if income increases by 50% and demand also rise by 50%, then the demand would be called unitary income elasticity of demand. In such a case, the numerical value of income elasticity of demand is equal to one ($e_y = 1$).

b. More than Unitary Income Elasticity of Demand:

This implies that positive income elasticity of demand would be more than unitary when the proportionate change in the quantity demanded is more than the proportionate change in income. For example, if the income increases by 50% and demand rise by 100%. In such a case, the numerical value of income elasticity of demand would be more than one ($e_y>1$).

c. Less than Unitary Income Elasticity of Demand:

Implies that positive income elasticity of demand would be less than unitary when the proportionate change in, the quantity demanded is less than proportionate change in income. For example, if the income increases by 50% and demand increase only by 25%. In such a case, the numerical value of income elasticity of demand would be less than one ($e_y<1$).

ii. Negative Income Elasticity of Demand:

This refers to a kind of income elasticity of demand in which the demand for a product decreases with an increase in consumer's income. The income elasticity of demand is nega

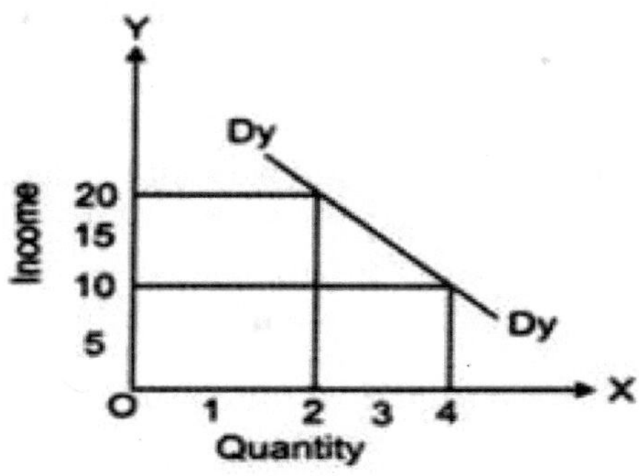

Fig: negative elasticity of demand

tive for inferior goods, also known as Giffen goods. For example, if the income of a consumer increases, he would prefer to purchase wheat instead of millet. In such a case, the millet would be inferior to wheat for the customer.

Negative income elasticity of demand is shown with the help of Figure:

Figure- shows that when income is Rs. 10, then the demand for goods is 4 units. On the other hand, when the income increases to Rs. 20, then the demand is 2 units. In Figure, the slope of the curve is downward from left to right, which indicates that the increase in income causes a decrease in demand and vice versa. Therefore, in such a case, the elasticity of demand is negative.

iii. Zero Income Elasticity of Demand:

Refers to the income elasticity of demand whose numerical value is zero. This is because there is no effect of the increase in consumer's income on the demand for the product. The income elasticity of demand is zero ($e_y = 0$) in the case of essential goods. For example, salt is demanded in the same quantity by a high-income and a low-income individual.

Figure- shows the zero income elasticity of demand:

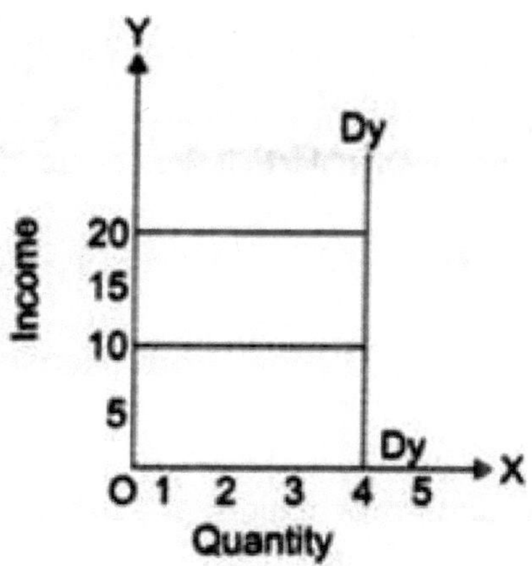

Fig: zero income elasticity of demand

Figure- shows that when income increases from Rs. 10 to Rs. 20, then the demand for goods remains the same, 4 units. In Figure-14, the slope of the curve is parallel to Y-axis (income side), which indicates that the increase in income causes no effect on demand. Therefore, in such a case, the elasticity of demand is zero.

Significance of Income Elasticity of Demand:

While price elasticity plays a significant role in the pricing of a product to maximize the total revenue of an organization in the short run, income elasticity of demand is important for production planning and management in the long run.

Following are some of the important uses of income elasticity of demand:

i. Helping in investment decisions:

Refers to one of the major significance of income elasticity of demand. In developing countries, such as India, the rate of growth of national income is not steady as it is in the case of developed countries. Moreover in developing countries, a rise in national income does not result in an immediate increase in the demand for certain goods.

The concept of national income is very important for sellers as it helps them to allocate their resources in different industries. Generally, sellers prefer to invest in industries where the demand for goods is more concerning proportionate change in the income or where the income elasticity of demand is greater than zero ($e_y > 1$).

For example, the demand for durable goods, such as vehicles, furniture, and electrical appliances, increases in response to an increase in the national income. In such industries, sellers earn high profits when there is an increase in national income. On the other hand, in industries with low-income elasticity ($e_y < 1$), there is a gradual increase in demand for goods, whereas the demand for goods having negative income elasticity declines when the national income grows.

ii. Forecasting demand:

This refers to the fact that income elasticity of demand help in anticipating the demand for goods in the future. If the change in income is certain, there would be a major change in the demand for goods. This is because if consumers are aware of the change in income, they may change their tastes and preferences for certain goods.

On the other hand, if the change in income is temporary, there would be a slow change in the demand. However, the demand for goods in the future is also influenced by various factors other than income.

iii. Categorizing goods:

Implies that income elasticity of demand helps in classifying goods, such as normal goods, essential goods, or inferior goods. The classification of goods enables sellers to select the goods to be produced and the number of goods to be produced. Apart from this, it also helps sellers to decide the income group to whom the goods should target.

Following assumptions are made while classifying goods:

a. A good would be a normal good if the income elasticity of demand is positive.

b. A good would be an inferior good if the income elasticity of demand is negative. For example, millet is inferior to wheat; therefore, the demand for millet is negative.

c. A good would be a luxury good, if the income elasticity of demand is positive and greater than one ($e_y > 1$). For example, the demand for cars and air conditioners is income elastic.

d. A good would be an essential good, if the income elasticity of demand is positive but less than one ($e_y < 1$). For example, food grains and clothes.

e. A good would be neutral if the income elasticity of demand is zero ($e_y=0$).

Cross Elasticity of Demand: Definitions, Types, and Measurement of Cross Elasticity of Demand!

It is the ratio of proportionate change in the quantity demanded of Y to a given proportionate change in the price of the related commodity X. It is a measure of relative change in the quantity demanded of a commodity due to a change in the price of its substitute/complement. It can be expressed as:

$$Ce \frac{\text{Proportionate change in the quantity demanded of Y}}{\text{Proportionate change in the price of X}}$$

Cross elasticity may be infinite or zero if the slightest change in the price of X causes a substantial change in the quantity demanded of Y. It is always the case with goods that have perfect substitutes for one another. Cross elasticity is zero if a change in the price of one commodity will not affect the quantity demanded of the other. In the case of goods that are not related to each other, the cross elasticity of demand is zero.

Definition:

"The cross elasticity of demand is the proportional change in the quantity of X good demanded resulting from a given relative change in the price of a related good Y" **Ferguson**

"The cross elasticity of demand is a measure of the responsiveness of purchases of Y to change in the price of X" **Leibafsky**

Types of Cross Elasticity of Demand:

1. Positive:

When goods are the substitute of each other then cross elasticity of demand is positive. In other words, when an increase in the price of Y leads to an increase in the demand for X. For instance, with the increase in the price of tea, the demand for coffee will increase.

In fig. quantity has been measured on OX-axis and price on OY-axis. At price OP of Y-commodity, the demand of X-commodity is OM. Now as the price of Y commodity increases to OP_1 demand of X-commodity increases to OM_1 Thus, cross elasticity of demand is positive.

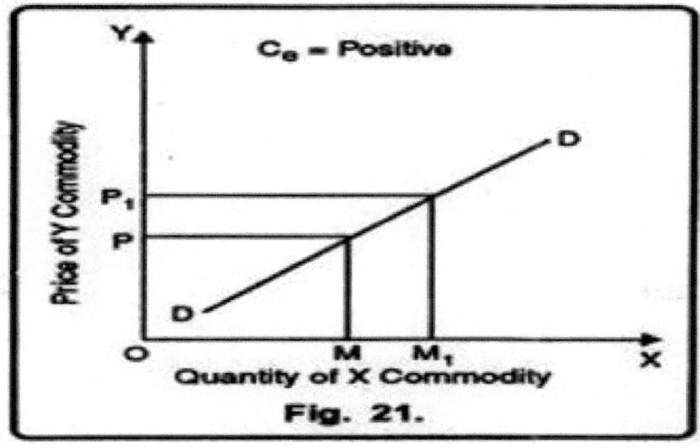

Fig: positive

2. Negative:

In the case of complementary goods, the cross elasticity of demand is negative. A proportionate increase in the price of one commodity leads to a proportionate fall in the demand of another commodity because both are demanded jointly. In fig. quantity has been measured on OX-axis while the price has been measured on OY-axis. When the price of commodity increases from OP to OP_1 quantity demanded falls from OM to OM_1. Thus, the cross elasticity of demand is negative.

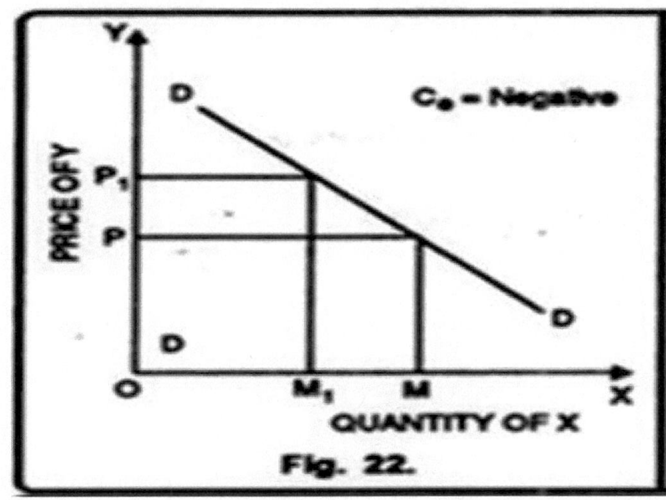

Fig: negative

3. Zero:

Cross elasticity of demand is zero when two goods are not related to each other. For instance, an increase in the price of the car does not affect the demand for cloth. Thus, the cross elasticity of demand is zero. It has been shown in fig.

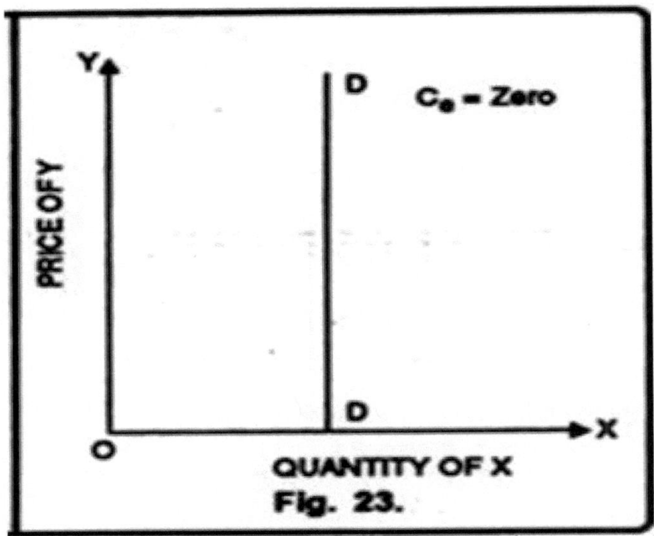

Fig: zero

Therefore, it depends upon the substitutability of goods. If substitutability is perfect, cross elasticity is infinite; if on the other hand, substitutability does not exist, cross elasticity is zero. In the case of complementary goods like jointly demanded goods cross elasticity is negative. A rise in the price of one commodity X will mean not only a decrease in the quantity of X but also a decrease in the quantity demanded of Y because both are demanded together.

Measurement of Cross Elasticity of Demand:

Cross elasticity of demand can be measured by the following formula:

$$EC = \frac{\text{Percentage change in quantity demanded of Good} - X}{\text{Percentage change in the price of Good} - Y}$$

$$= \frac{\dfrac{\text{Change in quantity demanded of X}}{\text{Original Quantity of X}} \times 100}{\dfrac{\text{Change in Price of Y}}{\text{Original Price of Y}} \times 100}$$

$$= \frac{\dfrac{\Delta Q_x}{Q_x}}{\dfrac{\Delta Q_y}{Q_y}} = \frac{\Delta Q_x}{Q_x} \times \frac{P_y}{\Delta P_y}$$

$$EC = \frac{P_y}{\Delta_n} \times \frac{\Delta Q_n}{\Delta P_y}$$

Where

Py = Original price of good-Y

ΔPy = Change in price of good-Y

Q_x = Original quantity demanded of X

ΔQ_x = Change in the quantity demanded of X

Demand Forecasting: Concept, Significance, Objectives, and Factors

An organization faces several internal and external risks, such as high competition, failure of technology, labor unrest, inflation, recession, and change in government laws.

Therefore, most of the business decisions of an organization are made under the conditions of risk and uncertainty.

An organization can lessen the adverse effects of risks by determining the demand or sales prospects for its products and services in the future. Demand forecasting is a systematic process that involves anticipating the demand for the product and services of an organization in the future under a set of uncontrollable and competitive forces.

Some of the popular definitions of demand forecasting are as follows:

According to Evan J. Douglas, “Demand estimation (forecasting) may be defined as a process of finding values for demand in future periods.”

In the words of **Cundiff and Still**, “Demand forecasting is an estimate of sales during a specified future period based on the proposed marketing plan and a set of particular uncontrollable and competitive forces.”

Demand forecasting enables an organization to take various business decisions, such as planning the production process, purchasing raw materials, managing funds, and deciding the price of the product. An organization can forecast demand by making own estimates called guess estimate or taking the help of specialized consultants or market research agencies. Let us discuss the significance of demand forecasting in the next section.

Law of Supply

Meaning of Supply

Supply is the quantity of a good which is offered for sale at a given price at a particular time. **"The amount of a product that firms are able and willing to offer for sale is called the quantity supplied."**

Supply is the desired flow. It measures how much firms are willing to sell and not how much they sell. It is to be remembered that the firms may not supply the entire amount of a commodity that they produce per period. Supply may exceed or fall short of production. Supply in a particular year is the total production plus minus stocks of the commodity.

It is observed in markets that when more prices of commodities are offered to sellers. They increase the quantity supplied of these commodities and when the level of prices decreases, the sellers decrease the quantity supplied. This behavior of the seller is called the law of supply.

Law of supply

Definition

"Other things remaining the same, if the price of a commodity increases its quantity supplied increases and if the price of a commodity decreases, quantity supplied also decreases".

There exists a direct and positive relationship between price and quantity supplied of a commodity. The functional relationship between quantity supplied and the price of a commodity can be expressed as:

$Q_s = f(P)$

Where Q_s = quantity supplied

P = price of the commodity

Assumptions: The assumptions of the law of supply are as under

No change in the cost of production

It assumed that there is no change in the cost of production because the profit decreases with the increase in the cost of production and it causes the decrease in supply. If the price of a commodity decreases and the cost of production also decreases, at the same time, the quantity supplied does not decrease and profit remains constant.

No change in technology

It is also assumed that technique of production does not change. If better methods of production are invented, profit increases at the previous price. The sellers increase supply and the law of supply does not operate.

No change in climate

It is also assumed that there is no change in the climatic situation. For example, at any place flood or earthquake occurred. The supply of goods decreases at that place at the previously prevailing price.

No change in prices of substitutes

If the prices of substitutes of a commodity fall then the tendency of consumers diverts to substitutes therefore, the supply of a commodity falls without any price change.

No change in natural resources

If the quantity of natural resources (minerals, gas, coal, oil, etc) increases, the cost of production decreases. It causes to increase in quantity supplied.

No change in the price of capital goods

The capital goods are raw materials, machinery, tools, etc. The cost of production increases due to an increase in the prices of capital goods. It can lead to a decrease in the quantity supplied.

No change in the political situation

The amount of investment is affected by the change in the political situation of a country. The production of goods decreases due to a decrease in investment.

No change in tax policy

It is also assumed that the taxation policy of the government does not change. The increase in taxes affects investment and production and the supply of goods decreases.

Explanation

The slope of the supply function i.e. $\Delta Q/\Delta P$ is positive. Regarding the assumptions, the standard supply function is written as $Q_s = - c + d P$

Where c and d are parameters while P and Q_s are independent and dependent variables, respectively. The positive sign represents a direct relationship between P and Q_s.

The supply function is expressed with the help of the following example: $Q_s = - 2 + 2 P$

By assuming different values of P, we can calculate the different values of Q_s as shown below.

Price (P)	Quantity supplied Q_s
0	-2
1	-0
2	2
3	4
4	6
5	8

Table representing supply function

As we assumed the different values of 'P' from zero to 5, then the calculated values of Qs increase from - 2 to 8.

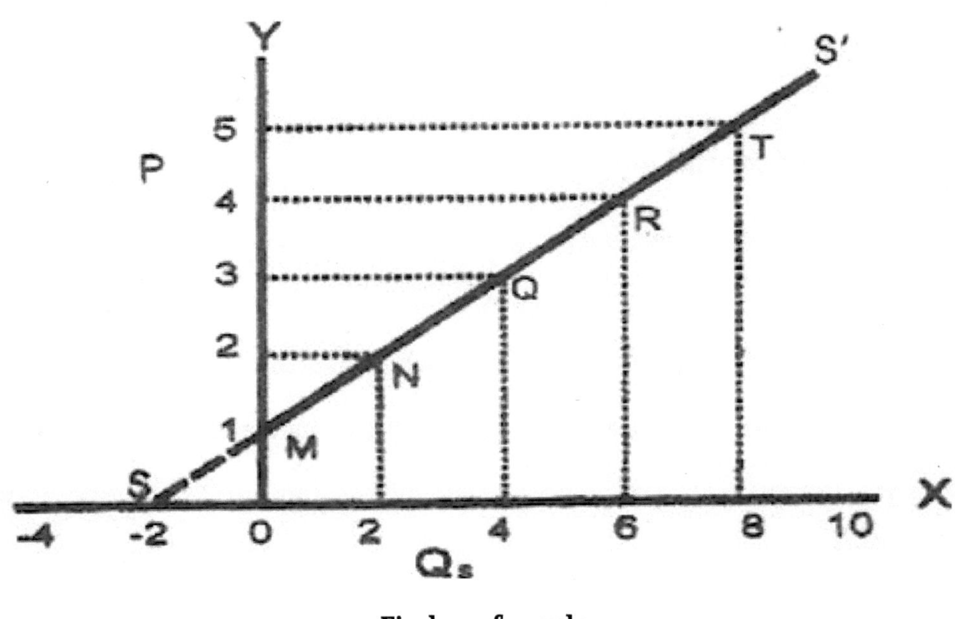

Fig: law of supply

The quantity supplied is expressed on X-axis while the price is measured on Y-axis. The law of supply can be illustrated through the supply schedule as shown in the above supply curve SS'. By plotting the various combinations of price and quantity supplied, we get different points S, M, N, Q, R, and T. by joining these points, we get our desired supply curve SS', having a positive slope as shown in the above figure.

Causes of the positive slope of the supply curve

Following are the causes of the positive slope of the supply curve.

Profit

When the price of a commodity increase, the seller increases the quantity supplied. The profit of the seller increases and the seller aims to profit maximization.

Cost of production

The cost of production increases due to an increase in quantity supplied. It is necessary to increases prices to maintain or increase the level of profit. Therefore, there is a direct relationship between price and quantity supplied.

Future Expectations

If there is a tendency of increasing prices at the present period, the sellers increase quantity supplied for the lust of profit. It may be expectations in future to decrease prices. Now they want to maximize their profit due to good present circumstances.

Determinants of Supply:

The supply of a commodity depends not only on the price of that commodity but also on other factors.

The supply function may now be expressed as: $S_x = f(P_x, P_a... P_c, P_L... P_O, T, C_r, S_t, O, G)$,

P_x → own price of good x,

ADVERTISEMENTS:

P_a ... P_c → prices of related goods,

P_L ... P_O→ prices of inputs,

T → time,

S_t → the state of technology,

O → objectives of the firm, and

G → taxes, subsidies, and regulation.

Now we will explain all these determinants of supply in brief:

(a) Own Price—$S_x = f(P_x)$:

Firstly, the most important factor that influences the supply of a commodity is its price. And the relationship between supply and own price is a direct one.

(b) Prices of Related Goods—$S_x = f(P_a \ldots P_c)$:

Secondly, the supply of any commodity largely depends not only on the own price of the commodity but also on the prices of its substitute and complementary goods.

If the market price of wheat rises, the jute farmers would be interested in wheat production so that in the next season they can increase the supply of wheat. On the other hand, in the case of a joint product, a rise in the market price of mutton will increase the quantity of leather supplied.

(c) Prices of Inputs—$S_x = f(P_L \ldots P_o)$:

Thirdly, the price of inputs is also an important determinant of supply. If the price of an input (say, wage bill) rises, the cost of production will surely increase. Consequently, profit will tend to decline. Seeing an unprofitable situation, a firm will reduce the supply of a commodity and will try to switch over to the production of another commodity that is still not unprofitable.

(d) Time—$S_x = f(T)$:

Fourthly, in the short run, usually the supply of a commodity (mainly perishable goods) is unresponsive to price change. But, in the long run, the supply of a commodity tends to be more flexible or fluctuating in response to the changing situation.

For non-reproducible goods, the supply becomes highly inelastic. One can now suggest that the supply of a commodity also depends on its nature. For instance, the supply of non-perishable goods responds more than the perishable goods when their prices change.

(e) Technology—$S_x = f(S_t)$:

Fifthly, the state of art or technology has an important bearing on the supply of a commodity. As newer and modern technologies are employed in a concern, production and productivity rise and average costs of production tend to decline. This results in a change in quantity supplied.

(f) Firm's Objectives—$S_x = f(O)$:

Sixthly, the nature of a firm's objectives also affects supply decisions. Firms can have different goals. Usually, profit maximization is the most fundamental objective of a firm. Modern business firms aim at maximization of sales revenue rather than profit.

(g) Government Policy—$S_x = f(G)$:

Finally, by imposing taxes on firms, the government can affect the supply of a commodity. The government may ask business firms to pay taxes for polluting the atmosphere or for meeting government services on education, health, etc. As these taxes increase costs, firms reduce supplies. Similarly, subsidies may be given to firms so that they can produce goods needed by society.

All these determinants of supply have been represented in a diagrammatic form (Figure):

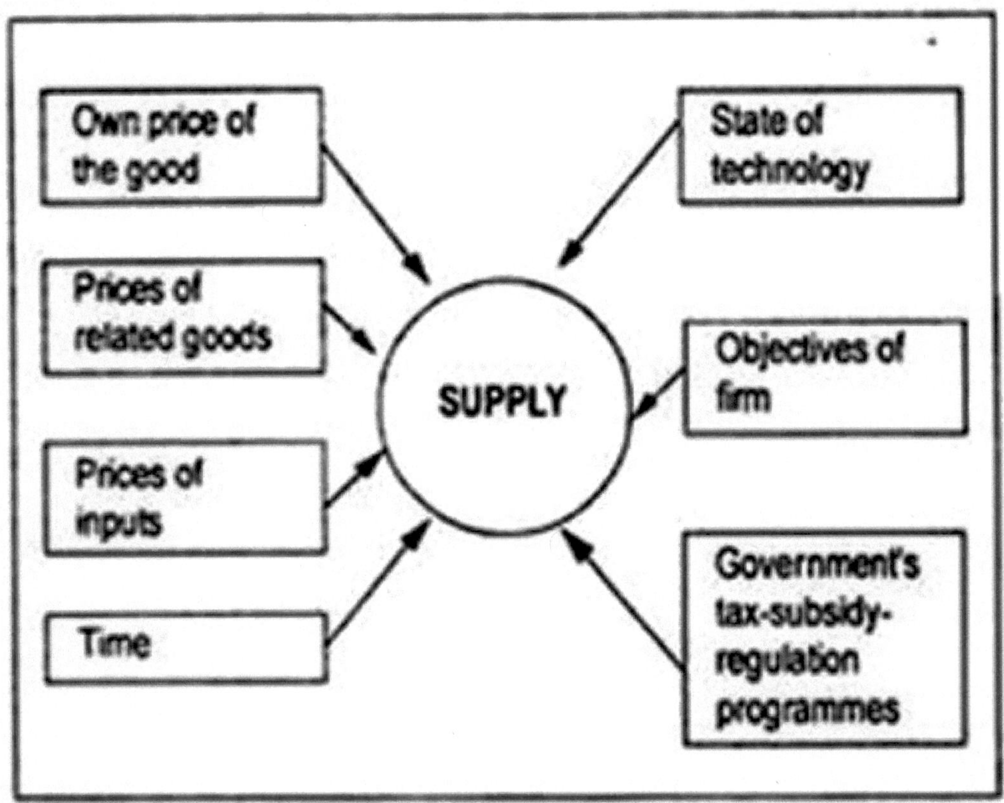

Fig: determinants of supply

3

THEORY OF PRODUCTION

THEORY OF PRODUCTION

Introduction

Production is the result of co-operation of four factors of production viz., land, labor, capital, and organization. This is evident from the fact that no single commodity can be produced without the help of any one of these four factors of production. Therefore, the producer combines all the four factors of production in a technical proportion. The producer aims to maximize his profit.

Meaning of Production Function

In simple words, production function refers to the functional relationship between the quantity of a good produced (output) and factors of production (inputs).

"The production function is purely a technical relation which connects factor inputs and output." **Prof. Koutsoyiannis**

Defined production function as " The relation between a firm's physical production (output) and the material factors of production (inputs). " **Prof. Watson**

Mathematically, such a basic relationship between inputs and outputs may be expressed as:

$$Q = f(L, C, N)$$

Where Q = Quantity of output

L = Labour

C = Capital

N = Land.

Hence, the level of output (Q), depends on the quantities of different inputs (L, C, N) available to the firm. In the simplest case, where there are only two inputs, labor (L) and capital (C) and one output (Q), the production function becomes.

$Q = f(L, C)$

Types of Production Function

Introduction: The production function depicts the relation between physical outputs of a production process and physical inputs, i.e. factors of production. The practical application of production functions is obtained by valuing the physical outputs and inputs by their prices. This is the principle of how the production function is made a practical concept, i.e. measurable and understandable in practical situations like

- Fixed proportion and variable proportion Production function
- Short period and long period Production function
- Cobb – Douglas Production function

Fixed Proportion Production Function

Definition: The Fixed Proportion Production Function, also known as a Leontief Production Function implies that fixed factors of production such as land, labor, raw materials are used to produce a fixed quantity of output and these production factors cannot be substituted for the other factors.

In other words, a fixed quantity of inputs is used to produce the fixed quantity of output. All the factors of production are fixed and cannot be substituted for one another. Suppose there are 50 workers required to produce 500 units of a product, then the technical Coefficient of production will be 1/10. In the case of a fixed proportion production function, this one-tenth of labor must be employed for the production of fixed output and no other factors of production can be substituted in place of labor.

The concept of fixed proportion production function can be further understood with the help of a figure as shown below:

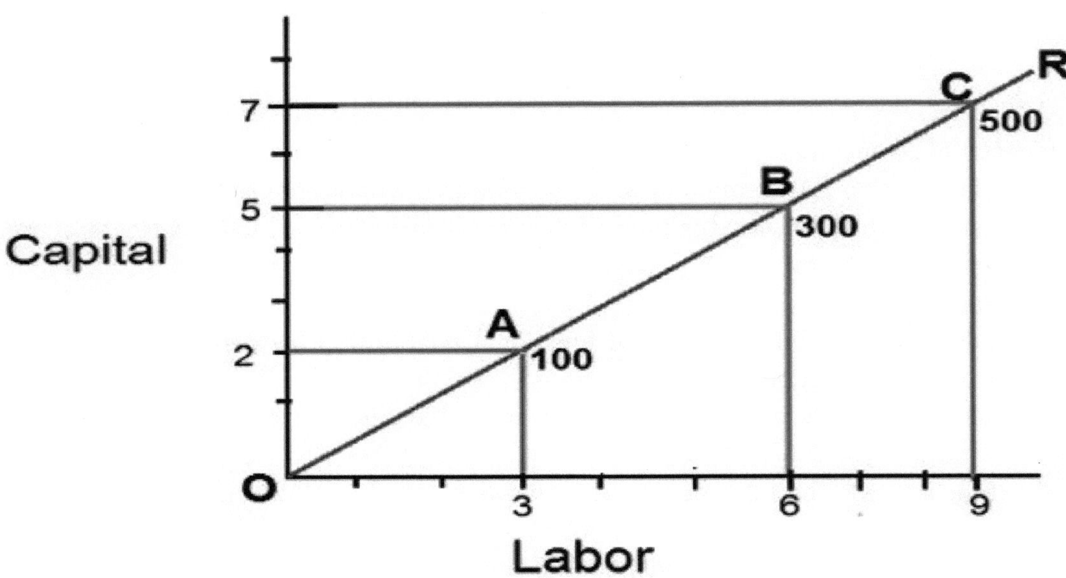

Fig: fixed labor-capital ratio

In the given figure, OR shows the fixed labor-capital ratio, if a firm wants to produce 100 units of a product, then 2 units of capital and 3 units of labor must be employed to attain this output.

Similarly, for the production of 300 and 500 units of a product, 5 units of capital and 6 units of labor and 7 units of capital and 9 units of labor must be employed respectively.

It may be noticed that along the isoquant curve the marginal product of a factor is zero, let's say, for the production of 300 units of a product, the capital is fixed (say 5 units), then any additional units of labor won't make any difference in the total production, hence, the marginal product of labor is zero.

Variable Proportion Production Function

Definition: The Variable Proportion Production Function implies that the ratio in which the factors of production such as labor and capital are used is not fixed, and it is variable. Also, the different combinations of factors can be used to produce the given quantity, thus, one factor can be substituted for the other.

In the case of the variable proportion production function, the technical Coefficient of production is variable, i.e. the required quantity of output can be achieved through the combination of different quantities of factors of production, such as these factors can be varied by substituting other factors/ factors in its place.

Suppose 40 workers are required to produce 200 units of a product, then the technical Coefficient of production will be 1/5. In the case of a variable proportion production function, one-fifth of labor is not necessarily to be employed, but the different combinations of factors of production can be used to produce a given level of output. Thus, the labor can be substituted for any other factors.

The concept of variable proportion production function can be further understood from an isoquant curve, as shown in the figure below.

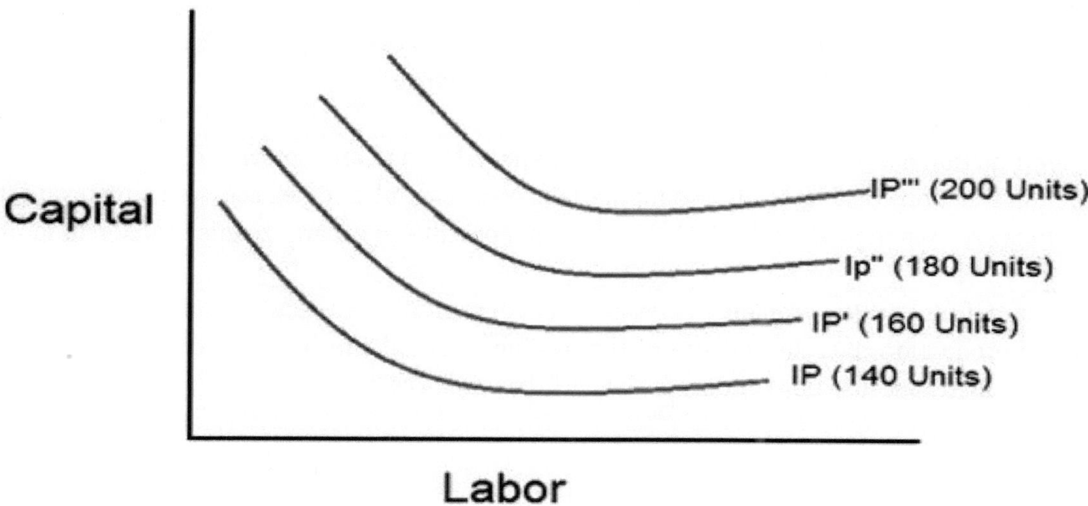

Fig: isoquant curves

In the figure, the isoquant curves show that the different combinations of factors of technical substitution can be employed to get the required amount of output. Thus, for the production of a given level of product, the input factors can be substituted for the other.

Short-run Production

A short-run production function refers to that time, in which the installation of a new plant and machinery to increase the production level is not possible

The short-run production function alludes to the time, in which at least one factor of production is fixed.

- Law of variable proportion
- No change in scale of production.
- Factor ratio changes
- There are barriers to entry and the firms can shut down but cannot fully exist.

Long-run production

The long-run production function is one in which the firm has got sufficient time to install new machinery or capital equipment, instead of increasing the labor units.

The long-run production function connotes the time, in which all the factors of production are variable.

- Law of returns to scale
- Change in the scale of production.
- Factor ratio does not change.
- Firms are free to enter and exit.

The Cobb-Douglas Production Function

The below-mentioned article provides a close view of the Cobb-Douglas Production Function.

The Cobb-Douglas production function is based on the empirical study of the American manufacturing industry made by Paul H. Douglas and C.W. Cobb. It is a linear homogeneous production function of degree one which takes into account two inputs, labor, and capital, for the entire output of the .manufacturing industry.

The Cobb-Douglas production function is expressed as:

$$Q = AL\alpha\ C\beta$$

Where Q is output and L and C are inputs of labor and capital respectively. A, a, and β are positive parameters where = a > O, β > O.

The equation tells that output depends directly on L and C, and that part of output which cannot be explained by L and C is explained by A which is the 'residual', often called technical change.

Criticisms of C-D Production Function:

The C-D production function has been criticized by Arrow, Chenery, Minhas, and Solow as discussed below:

1. The C-D production function considers only two inputs, labor, and capital, and neglects some important inputs, like raw materials, which are used in production. It is, therefore, not possible to generalize this function to more than two inputs.

2. In the C-D production function, the problem of measurement of capital arises because it takes only the quantity of capital available for production. But the full use of the available capital can be made only in periods of full employment. This is unrealistic because no economy is always fully employed.

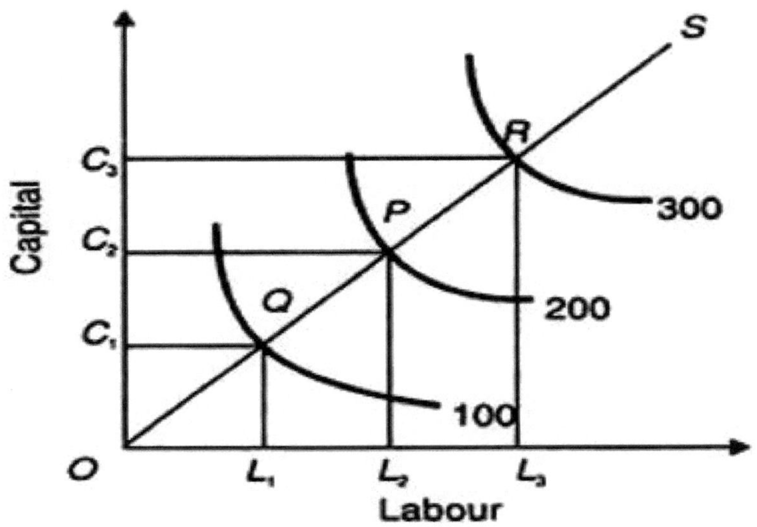

Fig: C-D production function

3. The C-D production function is criticized because it shows constant returns to scale. But constant returns to scale are not an actuality, for either increasing or decreasing returns to scale apply to production.

4. The C-D production function is based on the assumption of substitutability of factors and neglects the complementarity of factors.

5. This function is based on the assumption of perfect competition in the factor market which is unrealistic. If, however, this assumption is dropped, the coefficients α and β do not represent factor shares.

6. One of the weaknesses of C-D function is the aggregation problem. This problem arises when this function is applied to every firm in the industry and the entire industry. In this situation, there will be many production functions of low or high aggregation. Thus the C-D function does not measure what it aims at measuring.

Managerial uses of Production Function

Introduction

The production function developed in economic theory is a microeconomic concept. But the production function developed by Cobb-Douglas is a macroeconomic concept. The production function is concerned with explaining how the maximum quantity of output can you produced from the minimum quantities of inputs. The main uses of production function are

- To know the least-cost combination
- To maximize production
- To attain equilibrium
- Helps in decision-making
- The basis for production planning
- To know the least-cost combination

The production function analysis mentions how some factor inputs have to be kept constant and some other are varied to produce a given amount of output. But there are certain indivisible inputs like machinery, technical skill, etc,

- **To maximize production**

The knowledge of production functions is very much necessary to managers whenever they want to maximize production from given inputs. In this regard, they use the isoquant and is cost curve concepts to choose the optimum combination of factor inputs.

- **To attain equilibrium**

The producer like a consumer has to function in equilibrium. It is the responsibility of the management to produce a given quantity of output at a minimum cost. The management, to do so, has to equate the managerial rate of technical substitution with the price ratio of the two inputs.

- **Helps in decision making**

The production function is now being used in decision making, this analysis helps us to solve two important issues, namely (i) how to obtain maximum and output from a given set of inputs and (ii) how to obtain a given output from the minimum aggregation of inputs. With the development of linear programming in production, complex problems have been solved to a great extent.

- **The basis for production planning**

Production function serves as the basis of programming techniques in production planning. With the application of computers, the complex problems in production function are being solved to the satisfaction of the manager.

Law of Variable Proportions

Introduction

Law of Variable Proportions occupies an important place in economic theory. This law is also known as the Law of Proportionality. Keeping other factors fixed, the law explains the production function with a one-factor variable. In the short run when the output of a commodity is sought to be increased, the law of variable proportions comes into operation.

Definitions:

"As the proportion of the factor in a combination of factors is increased after a point, first the marginal and then the average product of that factor will diminish." **Benham**

Assumptions: Law of variable proportions is based on the following assumptions:

(i) Constant Technology:

The state of technology is assumed to be given and constant. If there is an improvement in technology the production function will move upward.

(ii) Factor Proportions are Variable:

The law assumes that factor proportions are variable. If factors of production are to be combined in a fixed proportion, the law has no validity.

(iii) Homogeneous Factor Units:

The units of variable factor are homogeneous. Each unit is identical in quality and amount with every other unit.

(iv) Short-Run:

The law operates in the short run when it is not possible to vary all factor inputs.

Explanation of the Law:

To understand the law of variable proportions we take the example of agriculture. Suppose land and labor are the only two factors of production.

By keeping land as a fixed factor, the production of variable factor i.e., labor can be shown with the help of the following table:

Table 1.

Units of Land	Units of Labour	Total Production	Average Production	Marginal Production
10 Acres	0	–	–	–
,,	1	20	20	20 } 1st stage MP > AP
,,	2	50	25	30
,,	3	90	30	40
,,	4	120	30	30 } AP = MP
,,	5	140	28	20 } 2nd stage
,,	6	150	25	10
,,	7	150	21.3	0 MP=0 and TP Maximum
,,	8	140	17.5	–10 } 3rd stage MP < 0

Table represents marginal production

Graphic Presentation:

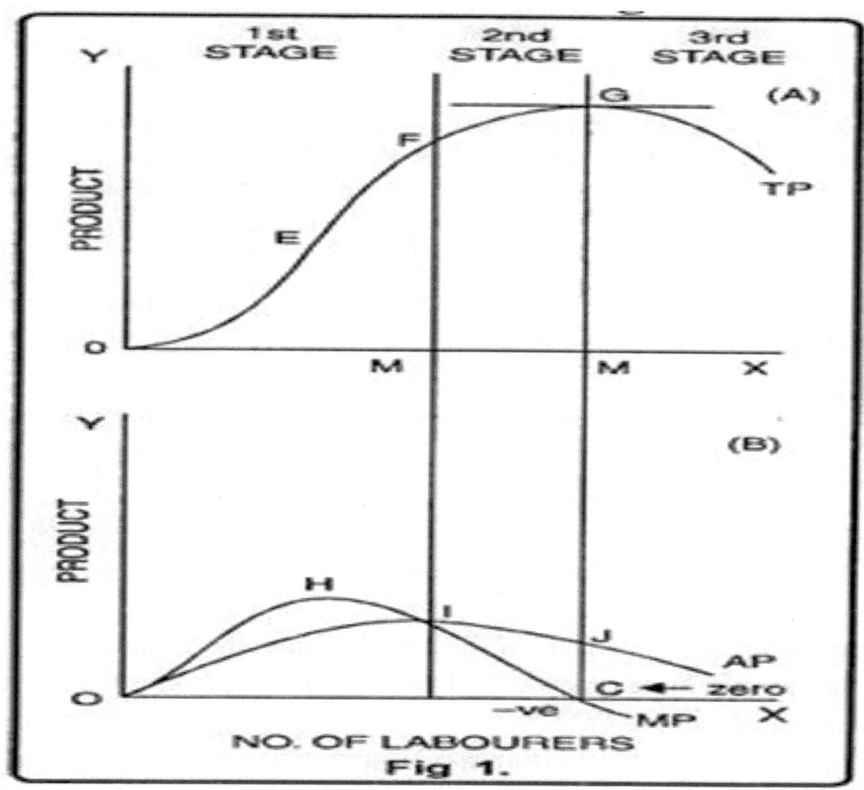

Fig 1.

Fig: three stages

Three Stages of the Law:

1. First Stage: The first stage starts from point 'O' and ends up to point F. At point F average product is maximum and is equal to the marginal product. In this stage, the total product increases initially at an increasing rate up to point E. between 'E' and 'F' it increases at a diminishing rate. Similarly, the marginal product also increases initially and reaches its maximum at point 'H'. Later on, it begins to diminish and becomes equal to the average product at point T. In this stage, the marginal product exceeds the average product (MP > AP).

2. Second Stage: It begins from point F. In this stage, the total product increases at a diminishing rate and is at its maximum at point 'G' correspondingly marginal product diminishes rapidly and becomes 'zero' at point 'C'. The average product is maximum at point 'I' and thereafter it begins to decrease. In this stage, marginal product is less than average product (MP < AP).

Total Product	Marginal Product	Average Product
Stage I First increases at increasing rate then at diminishing rate.	Increases in the beginning then reaches a maximum and begins to decrease.	First increases, continues to increase and becomes maximum.
Stage II Continues to increase at diminishing rate and becomes maximum.	Continues to diminish and becomes equal to zero.	Becomes equal to MP and then begins to diminish.
Stage III Diminishes	Becomes negative.	Continues to diminish but will always be greater than zero.

Table represents three stages

3. Third Stage: This stage begins beyond point 'G'. Here total product starts diminishing. The average product also declines. The marginal product turns negative. The Law of diminishing returns firmly manifests itself. In this stage, no firm will produce anything. This happens because the marginal product of the labor becomes negative. The employer will suffer losses by employing more units of laborers. However, of the three stages, a firm will like to produce up to any given point in the second stage only.

Condition or Causes of Applicability:

Many causes are responsible for the application of the law of variable proportions.

They are as follows:

1. Under Utilization of Fixed Factor:

In the initial stage of production, fixed factors of production like land or machine, are under-utilized. More units of variable factors, like labor, are needed for its proper utilization.

2. Fixed Factors of Production.

The foremost cause of the operation of this law is that some of the factors of production are fixed during a short period. When the fixed factor is used with the variable factor, then its ratio compared to the variable factor falls.

3. Optimum Production:

After making the optimum use of a fixed factor, then the marginal return of such variable factor begins to diminish. The simple reason is that after the optimum use, the ratio of fixed and variable factors become defective.

4. Imperfect Substitutes:

Mrs. Joan Robinson has put the argument that imperfect substitution of factors is mainly responsible for the operation of the law of diminishing returns. One factor cannot be used in place of the other factor.

Applicability of the Law of Variable Proportions:

The law of variable proportions is universal as it applies to all fields of production. This law applies to any field of production where some factors are fixed and others are variable. That is why it is called the law of universal application.

1. Application to Agriculture:

With a view of raising agricultural production, labor and capital can be increased to any extent but not the land, being fixed factor.

2. Application to Industries:

To increase the production of manufactured goods, factors of production have to be increased. It can be increased as desired for a long period, being variable factors.

Producer's Equilibrium

Introduction: The value of all assets used for production is limited. Hence, the producer has to use such a combination of inputs as would provide him with maximum output and profits. This optimum level of production, also called producer's equilibrium, is achieved when maximum output is derived from minimum costs.

Producer's Equilibrium: Economic production is the result of the output we produce by employing factors like land, labor, capital, and entrepreneurship. It is possible to determine the optimum amount of production possible considering different combinations of these inputs. Such a determination is called the producer's equilibrium.

There are two methods for the determination of Producer's Equilibrium:

1. Total Revenue and Total Cost Approach (TR-TC Approach)
2. Marginal Revenue and Marginal Cost Approach (MR-MC Approach)

It must be noted that the scope of the syllabus is restricted to "Producer's Equilibrium by MR- MC Approach". Still, for better understanding, "Producer's Equilibrium by TR-TC approach" is given. The producer can attain the equilibrium level under two different situations:

(i) When Price remains Constant (It happens under Perfect Competition). In this situation, the firm has to accept the same price as determined by the industry. It means any quantity of a commodity can be sold at that particular price.

(ii) When Price Falls with the rise in output (It happens under Imperfect Competition). In this situation, the firm follows its pricing policy. However, it can increase sales only by reducing the price.

Total Revenue-Total Cost Approach (TR-TC Approach): A firm attains the stage of equilibrium when it maximizes its profits, i.e. when it maximizes the difference between TR and TC. After reaching such a position, there will be no incentive for the producer to increase or decrease the output and the producer will be said to be at equilibrium.

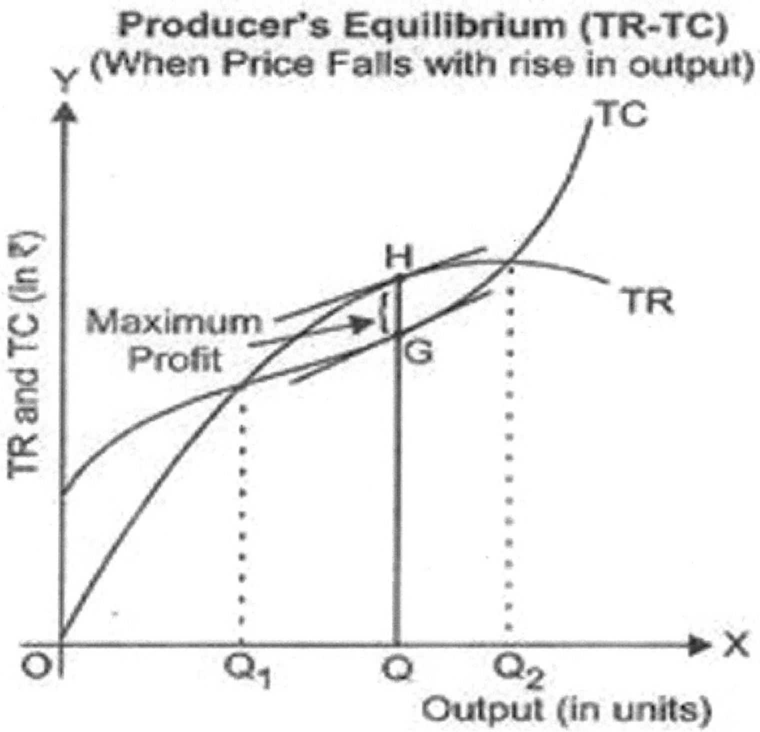

Fig: producers equilibrium(TR-TC)

Producer's Equilibrium is determined at OQ level of output corresponding to point K as at this point: (i) MC = MR; and (ii) MC is greater than MR after MC = MR output level. In Fig. 8.3, the output is shown on the X-axis and revenue and costs on the Y-axis. Both AR and MR curves are straight lines parallel to the X-axis. MC curve is U-shaped. Producer's equilibrium will be determined at OQ level of output corresponding to point K because only at point K, the following two conditions are met:

1. MC = MR; and
2. MC is greater than MR after MC = MR output level

than

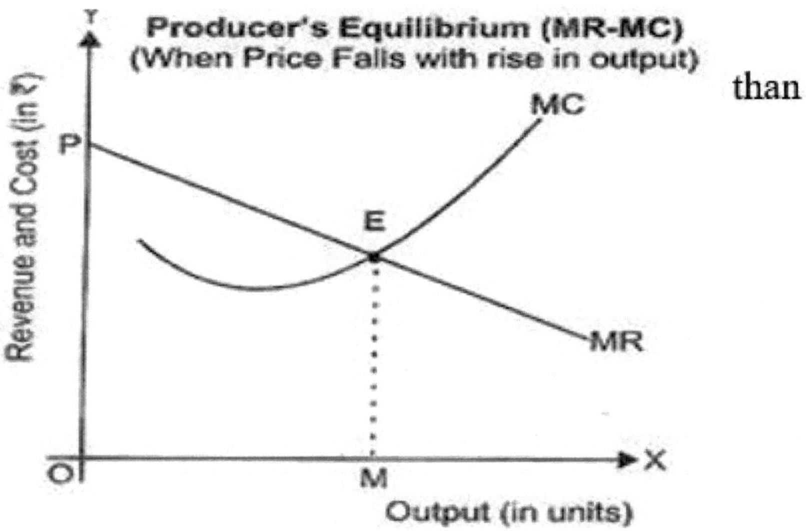

Fig: producers equilibrium(MR-MC)

Isoquant Curves: These lines represent various input combinations that produce the same levels of output. The producer can choose any of these combinations available to him because their outputs are always the same. Thus, we can also call them equal-product curves or production indifference curves.

Consider the table below. It shows four combinations, i.e. A, B, C, and D, which produce varying levels of output.

Factor combinations	Units of Labour	Units of Capital
A	5	9
B	10	6
C	15	4
D	20	3

Table representing levels of output

Plotting these figures on a graph provides us with this curve (Figure):

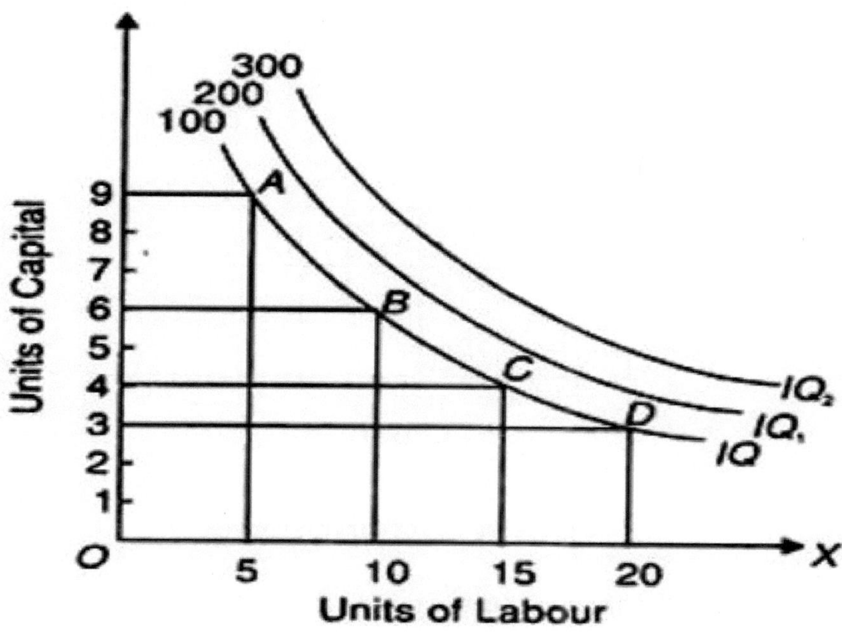

Fig: units of labour

The X-axis shows units of labor, while the Y-axis represents units of capital. Points A, B, C, and D are combinations of factors on which IQ is the level of output, i.e. 100 units. IQ1 and IQ2 represent the greater potential output.

Properties of Iso-quant Curve

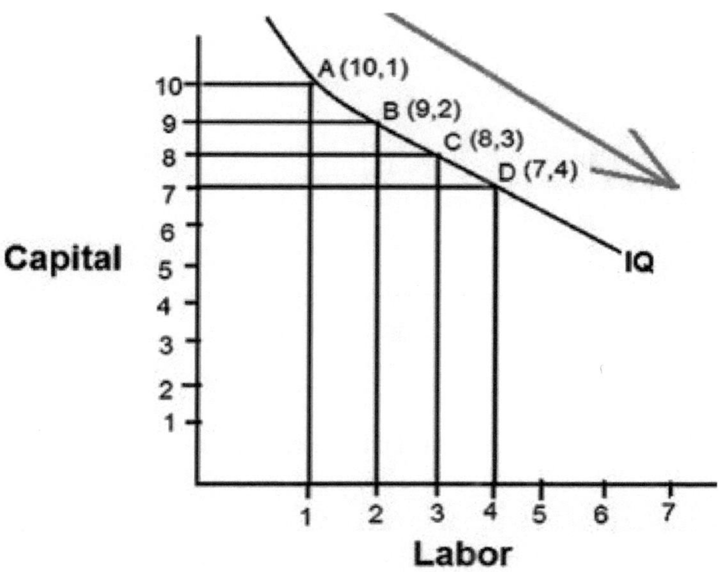

Fig: the iso-quant curve is negatively sloped

The iso-quant curve is negatively sloped, which means, to have the same level of production, the more use of units of one input factor is to be offset with the lesser units of another input factor. This complies with the principle of Marginal Rate of Technical Substitution (MRTP). For example, with more units of capital, the lesser units of labor are to be employed to have the same level of output. In the figure, it is clear that the reduction in capital is to be set off with the increase in labor, and thus, the IQ is negatively sloped.

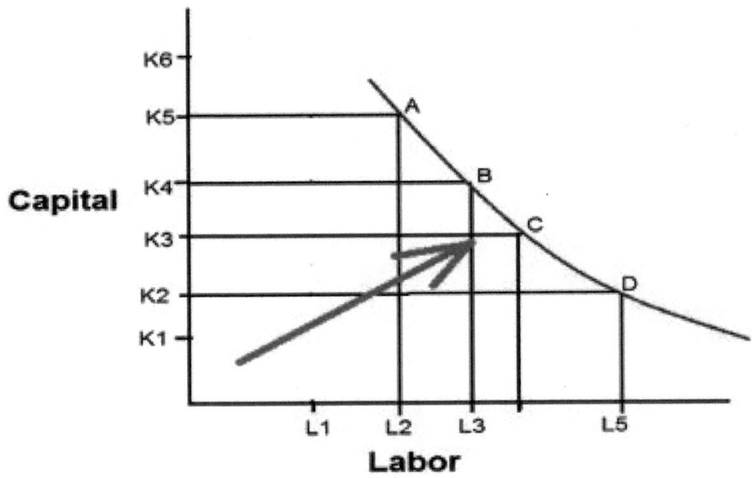

Fig: the iso-quant curve is convex

The iso-quant curve is convex to the origin because of the MRTP effect. This shows that factors of production are substitutable for each other and with the increase in one factor the other has to be reduced to have the same level of production.

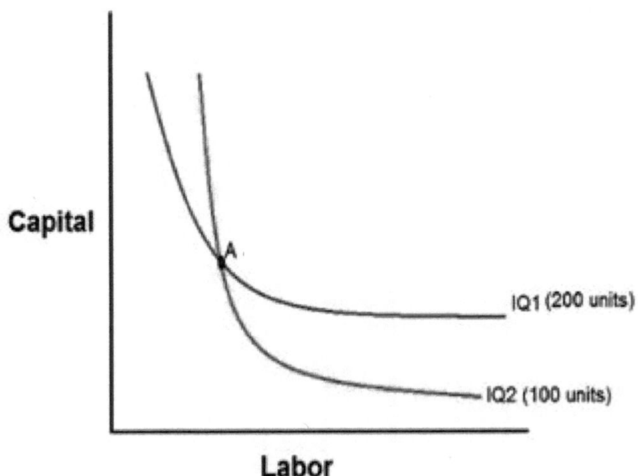

Fig: iso-quant curves cannot intersect

Iso-quant curves cannot intersect or be tangent to each other. If these intersects, then the results will be incorrect. A common factor combination on both the curves will show the same level of output, which is not feasible.

As per the figure, at point A, different combinations on IQ1 and IQ2 produce the same level of output which is not feasible. Since both, the curves show different levels of output i.e. 100 and 200 units respectively.

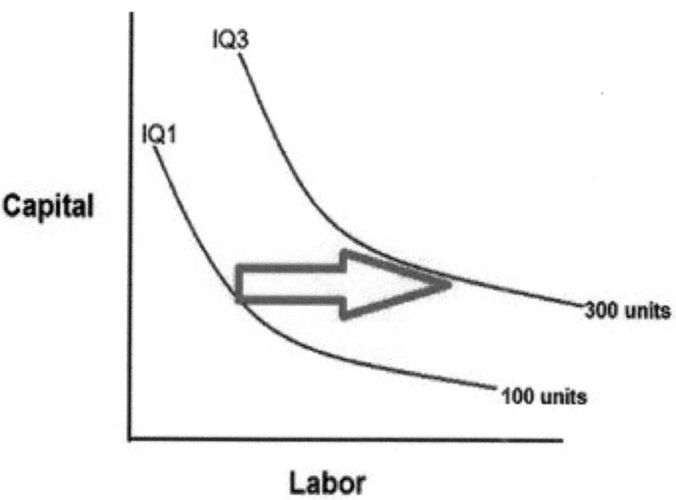

Fig: upper iso-quant curves yield higher outputs

Upper iso-quant curves yield higher outputs. This is possible because, at a higher curve, more factors of production are employed either the capital or the labor, which results in more production. The arrow in the figure shows an increase in the output with a right and upward shift of an iso-quant curve.

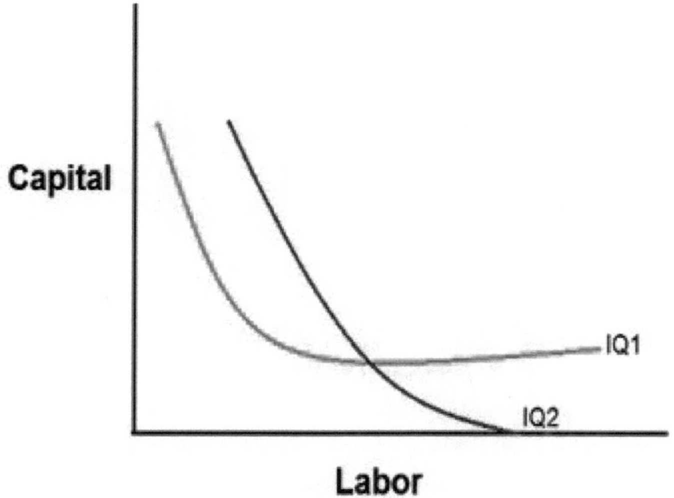

Fig: no iso-quant curve touches either of axis

No iso-quant curve touches either of the axis, X or Y. If it does so, then the rate of technical substitution would be void since it will show that a single factor is producing the given level of output without any units of other factor being employed.

As per the figure, if an iso-quant curve IQ2 touches the X-axis, this means no units of labor are employed, and only capital is required to produce the given level of output, which is not correct.

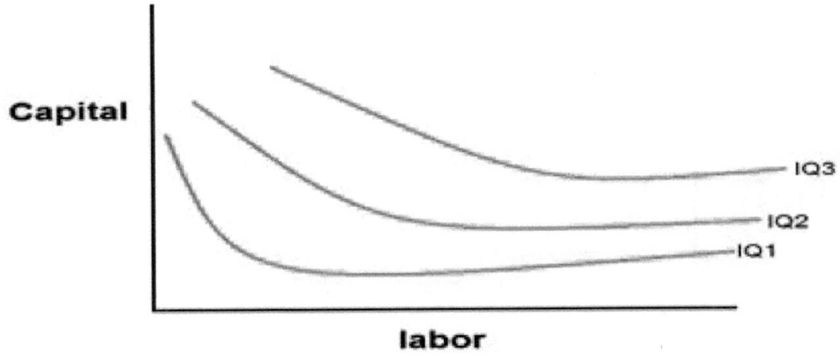

Fig: iso-quant curves need to be parallel to each other

Iso-quant curves need not be parallel to each other because the rate of technical substitution between the factors may vary in all the iso-quant curves.

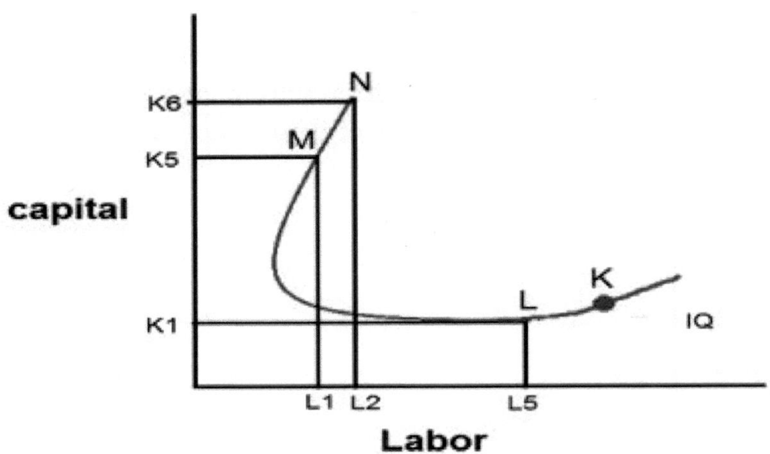

Fig: each iso-quant is oval-shaped

Each iso-quant curve is oval-shaped, which enables a firm to identify the most efficient factor of production. In the figure, point N and M show the same level of output with different combinations of labor and capital. Similarly, the combination at point K can be ruled out because of the positive slope. This means that, with an increase in labor, more capital is to be employed to have a constant production.

Conclusion: Hence, it is clear from the properties of an iso-quant curve that a firm can have the same level of production with different combinations of labor and capital that must be utilized in such a way that the overall profitability of the firm increases.

Isocost Lines

Isocost lines represent combinations of two factors that can be bought with different outlays. In other words, it shows how we can spend money on two different factors to produce maximum output. These lines are also called budget lines or budget constraint lines.

Properties of Iso cost:

1. Isocost line shows various combinations of inputs that a firm can purchase or hire at a given cost. By the use of isocosts and isoquants, a firm can determine the optimal input combination to maximize profit.

2. It is a graphical representation of various combinations of inputs say Labor(L) and capital (K) which give an equal level of output per unit of time. Output produced by different combinations of L and K is say, Q, then Q=f (L, K).

A higher isoquant refers to a larger output, while a lower isoquant refers to a smaller output.

3. Isocost line Suppose a firm uses only labor and capital in production. The total cost or expenditures of the firm can be represented by: C = wL + rK

4. In the Isocost line There are two-factor inputs labor and capital, the proportions of factors are variable, physical production conditions are given and the state of technology remains constant

5. Slope of isoquant = - MPL / MPK • Slope of is cost = PL / PK • For cost minimization we set these equal and rearrange to obtain: •

The Choice of Optimal Expansion Path

Introduction: The choice of optimal expansion path refers to the combinations of factors of production that enable the firm to produce various levels of output at the least cost while relative factor prices remain constant. Its analysis is done concerning the short run and the long run.

Assumptions:

This analysis is based on the following assumptions:

(1) There are two factors of production, labor, and capital, which are variable.

(2) All units of labor and capital are homogeneous.

(3) The price of labor (w) is constant.

(4) The price of capital (r) is constant.

(5) The firm increases its total outlay to expand its output.

Optional Choice of Inputs

A producer may maximize his profit in four ways. They are

- A producer can either minimize the cost of production for any given level of output.
- Maximize the output at any given level of outlay.
- Expansion path
- Cost minimization

Hence, we can once again say that the producer will be in equilibrium at the point where the slope of the isoquant is equal to the slope of isocost.

$$\text{i.e. Slope of isoquant} = \frac{\text{price of labor}}{\text{price of capital}}$$

Expansion path

Given these assumptions, to maximize its profits or to have the least cost combination, the firm combines labor and capital in such a way that the ratio of their MP is equal to the ratio of their prices, i.e., MPL/MPK = w/ r. This equality occurs at the point of tangency between an isocost line and an isoquant curve.

This is explained in Figure 18, where C1L1 C2L2 and C3L3are the different isocost lines. Line C2L2shows a higher total outlay than line C1L1 and C3L3 still a higher total outlay than line C2L2. They are shown parallel to each other thereby reflecting constant factor prices. There are three isoquants 100, 200, and 300 representing successively higher levels of output.

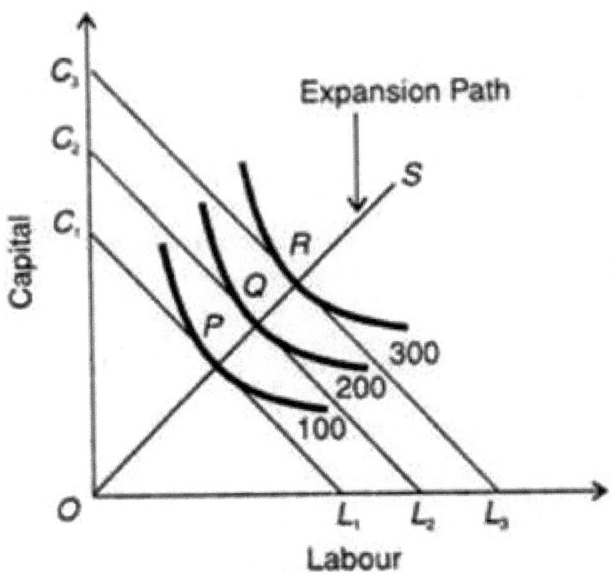

Fig: expansion path

The firm is in equilibrium at point P where the isoquant 100 is tangent to its corresponding isocost line C1L1 and similarly the other two isoquants 200 and 300 are tangent to isocost lines C2L2and C3L3 respectively at points Q and R. Each point of tangency implies the optimal combination of labor and capital that produces an optimal output level. The line OS joining these equilibrium points P, Q, and R through the origin is the expansion path of the firm. The firm expands its output along this line keeping factor prices constant.

Law of returns to scale

Introduction: In the long run all factors of production are variable. No factor is fixed. Accordingly, the scale of production can be changed by changing the quantity of all factors of production.

Definition:

"The term returns to scale refers to the changes in output as all factors change by the same proportion." **Koutsoyiannis**

"Returns to scale relates to the behavior of total output as all inputs are varied and is a long-run concept". **Leibhafsky**

Returns to scale are of the following three types:

1. Increasing Returns to scale.
2. Constant Returns to Scale
3. Diminishing Returns to Scale

Explanation:

In the long run, the output can be increased by increasing all factors in the same proportion. Generally, laws of returns to scale refer to an increase in output due to an increase in all factors in the same proportion. Such an increase is called returns to scale.

Suppose, initially production function is as follows:

P = f (L, K)

Now, if both the factors of production i.e., labor and capital are increased in the same proportion i.e., x, product function will be rewritten as.

Table 8. Showing different stages of return to scale

Units of Labour	Units of capital	%age increase in Labour & Capital	Total Product	%age increase in TP	Returns to scale
1	3	–	10	–	
2	9	100%	30	200%	Increasing
3	9	50%	60	100%	
4	12	33%	80	33%	Constant
5	15	25%	100	25%	
6	18	20%	120	10%	Decreasing
7	21	16.6%	130	8.3%	

Table represents different stages of return to scale

The above-stated table explains the following three stages of returns to scale:

1. Increasing Returns to Scale:

Increasing returns to scale or diminishing cost refers to a situation when all factors of production are increased, output increases at a all inputs are doubled, the output will also increase at a faster rate than double. Hence, it is said to be increasing returns to scale. This increase is due to many reasons like division external economies of scale. Increasing returns to scale can be illustrated with the help of diagram .

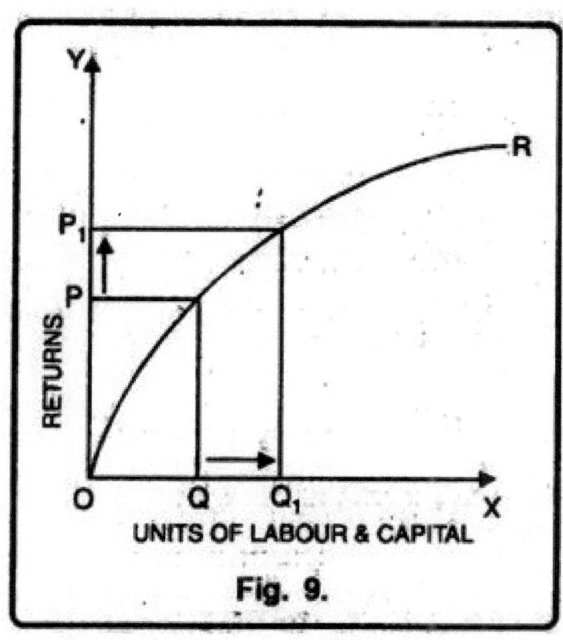

Fig: increasing returns to sales

In figure , the OX axis represents the increase in labor and capital while OY axis shows the increase in output. When labor and capital increase from Q to Q1, output also increases from P to P1 which is higher than the factors of production i.e. labor and capital.

2. Diminishing Returns to Scale:

Diminishing returns or increasing costs refer to that production situation, where if all the factors of production are increased in a given proportion, output increases in a smaller proportion. It means, if inputs are doubled, the output will be less than doubled.

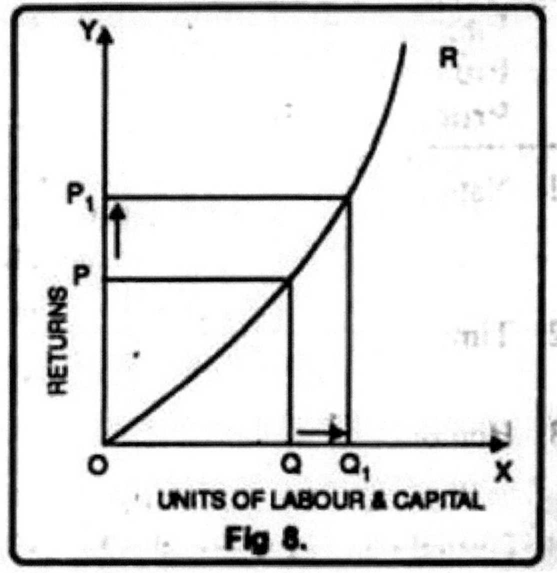

Fig: diminishing returns to scale

If 20 percent increase in labor and capital is followed by 10 percent increase in output, then it is an instance of diminishing returns to scale.

3. Constant Returns to Scale:

Constant returns to scale or constant cost refer to the production situation in which output increases exactly in the same proportion in which factors of production are increased. In simple terms, if factors of production are doubled output will also be doubled.

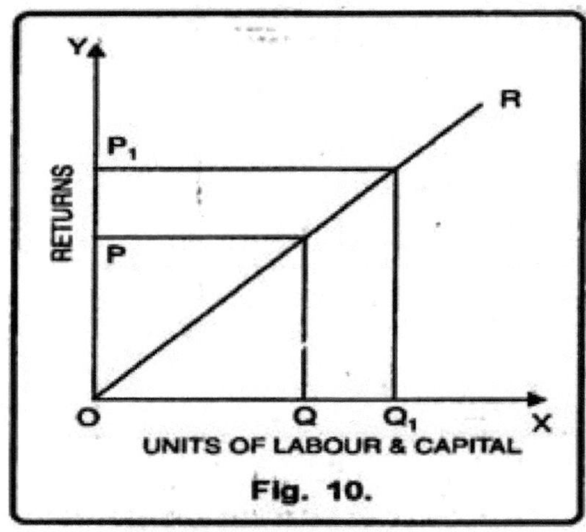

Fig: constant returns to scale

In this case, internal and external economies are exactly equal to internal and external diseconomies. This situation arises when after reaching a certain level of production, economies of scale are balanced by diseconomies of scale. This is known as the homogeneous production function.

Economies of Scale: Internal and External

Prof. Stigler defines economies of scale as synonyms with returns to scale. As the scale of production is increased, up to a certain point, one gets economies of scale. Beyond that, there are its diseconomies to scale Marshall has classified economies to scale into two parts as under:

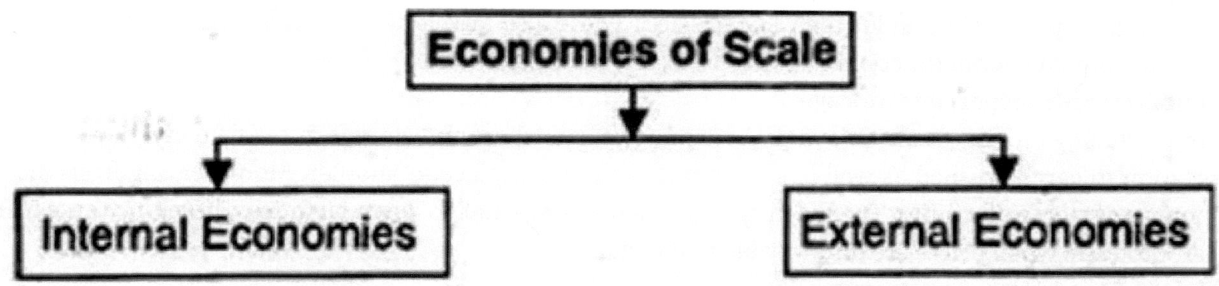

I.Internal Economies:

As a firm increases its scale of production, the firm enjoys several economies named internal economies. Internal economies are those which are special to each firm. For example, one firm will enjoy the advantage of good management; the other may have the advantage of specialization in the techniques of production and so on.

"Internal economies are those which are open to a single factory, or a single firm independently of the action of other firms. These result from an increase in the scale of output of a firm and cannot be achieved unless output increases." **Cairncross**

These economies are of the following types:

1. Technical Economies:

Technical economies influence the size of the firm. Generally, these economies accrue to large firms which enjoy higher efficiency from capital goods or machinery. Bigger firms having more resources at their disposal can install the most suitable machinery.

Technical economies are of three kinds:

(i) Economies of Dimension:

A firm by increasing the scale of production can enjoy the technical economies. When a firm increases its scale of production, the average cost of production falls but its average return will be more.

(ii) Economies of Linked Process:

A big firm can also enjoy the economies of linked processes. A big firm carries all productive activities. These activities get economies. These linked activities save time and transport costs to the firm.

(iii) Economies of the Use of By-Products:

All the large-sized firms are in a position to use their by-products and waste-material to produce another material and thus, supplement their income. For instance, sugar industries make power, alcohol out of the molasses.

2. Marketing Economies:

When the scale of production of a firm is increased, it enjoys numerous selling or marketing economies. In the marketing economies, we include advertisement economies, opening up of showrooms, the appointment of sole distributors, etc. Moreover, a large firm can conduct its research to effect improvement in the quality of the product and to reduce the cost of production. The other economies of scale are advertising economies, economies from special arrangements with exclusive dealers. In this way, all these acts lead to economies of large-scale production.

3. Labour Economies:

As the scale of production is expanded their accrue many labor economies, like new inventions, specialization, time-saving production, etc. A large firm employs a large number of workers. Each worker is given the kind of job he is fit for. The personnel .officer evaluates the working efficiency of the labor if possible. Workers are skilled in their operations which save production, time and simultaneously encourage new ideas.

4. Managerial Economies:

Managerial economies refer to production in managerial costs and proper management of the large-scale firm. Under this, work is divided and subdivided into different departments. Each department is headed by an expert who keeps a vigil on the minute details of his department. A small firm cannot afford this specialization. Experts can reduce the costs of production under their supervision. These also arise due to specialization of management and mechanization of managerial functions.

5. Economies of Transport and Storage:

A firm producing on large scale enjoys the economies of transport and storage. A big firm can have its means of transportation to carry finished as well as raw material from one place to another. Moreover, big firms also enjoy the economies of storage facilities. The big firm also has its storage and go down facilities. Therefore, these firms can store their products when prices are unfavorable in the market.

Pecuniary Economies:

Pecuniary economies are those which can be had after paying fewer prices for the factors used in the process of production and distribution. Big firms can get raw materials at a low price because they buy the same in the large bulk. In the same way, they enjoy a lot of concessions in bank borrowing and advertisements.

These economies occur to a large firm in the following:

(i) The firms producing output on a large scale purchase raw material in bulk quantity. As a result of this, the firms get a special discount from suppliers. This is a monetary gain to the firms.

These economies occur to a large firm in the following:

(i) The firms producing output on a large scale purchase raw material in bulk quantity. As a result of this, the firms get a special discount from suppliers. This is a monetary gain to the firms.

(ii) The large-scale firms are offered loans by the banks at a low interest rate and other favorable terms.

(iii) The large-scale firms are offered concessional transportation facilities by the transport companies because of the large-scale transportation handling.

(iv) The large-scale firms advertise their products on large scales and they are offered advertising facilities at lower prices by advertising firms and newspapers.

II. External Economies:

External economies refer to all those benefits which accrue to all the firms operating in a given industry. Generally, these economies accrue due to the expansion of industry and other facilities expanded by the Government.

According **to Cairncross**, "External economies are those benefits which are shared by several firms or industries when the scale of production in any industry increases."

1. Economies of Concentration:

As the number of firms in an area increases each firm enjoys some benefits like transport and communication, availability of raw materials, research and invention, etc. Further, financial assistance from banks and non-bank institutions easily accrues to the firm.

We can, therefore, conclude that the concentration of industries leads to economies of concentration.

2. Economies of Information:

When the number of firms in an industry expands they become mutually dependent on each other. In other words, they do not feel the need for independent research on an individual basis. Many scientific and trade journals are published. These journals provide information to all the firms which relate to new markets, sources of raw materials, latest techniques of production, etc.

3. Economies of Disintegration:

As an industry develops, all the firms engaged in it decide to divide and sub-divide the process of production among themselves. Each firm specializes in its process. For instance, in the case of the moped industry, some firms specialize in rims, hubs, and still others in chains, pedals, tires, etc. It is of two types-horizontal disintegration and vertical disintegration.

Significance of Economies of Scale:

The significance of economies of scale is discussed as under:

(a). Nature of the Industry:

The foremost significance of economies of scale is that it plays an important role in determining the nature of the industry i.e. increasing cost industry, constant cost industry, or decreasing cost industry.

(b). Analysis of Cost of Production:

When an industry expands in response to an increase in demand for its products, it experiences some external economies as well as some external diseconomies. The external economies tend to reduce the costs of production and thereby causing an upward shift in the long period average cost curve, whereas the external diseconomies tend to raise the costs and thereby causing an upward shift in the long period average cost curve.

Diseconomies of Scale of Production: Internal and External

The word diseconomies refer to all those losses which accrue to the firms in the industry due to the expansion of their output to a certain limit. These diseconomies arise due to the use of unskilled laborers, outdated methods of production, etc.

Like economies, diseconomies are also of two types.

1. Internal Diseconomies
2. External Diseconomies

1. Internal Diseconomies:

Internal diseconomies imply all those factors which raise the cost of production of a particular firm when its output increases beyond a certain limit. These factors may be of the following two types:

(a) Inefficient Management:

The main cause of the internal diseconomies is the lack of efficient or skilled management. When a firm expands beyond a certain limit, it becomes difficult for the manager to manage it efficiently or to coordinate the process of production.

(b) Technical Difficulties:

Another major reason for the onset of internal diseconomies is the emergence of technical difficulties. In every firm, there is an optimum point of technical economies

(c) Production Diseconomies:

The diseconomies of production manifest themselves when the expansion of a firm's production leads to a rise in the cost per unit of output.

(d) Marketing Diseconomies:

After an optimum scale, the further rise in the scale of production is accompanied by selling diseconomies. It is due to many reasons like advertisement expenditure is bound to increase more than proportionately.

(e) Financial Diseconomies:

If the scale of production increases beyond the optimum scale, the cost of financial capital rises. It may be due to relatively more dependence on external finances.

(f) Marketing Diseconomies:

After an optimum scale, the further rise in the scale of production is accompanied by selling diseconomies. It is due to many reasons like the overheads of marketing increase more than

2. External Diseconomies:

External diseconomies are not suffered by a single firm but by the firms operating in a given industry. These diseconomies arise due to much concentration and localization of industries beyond a certain stage. Localization leads to increased demand for transport and, therefore, transport costs rise. Similarly, as the industry expands, there is competition among firms for the factors of production and the raw materials. This raises the prices of raw materials and other factors of production. As a result of all these factors, external diseconomies become more powerful. Some of the external diseconomies are as under:

(a). Diseconomies of Pollution:

The localization of an industry in a particular place or region pollutes the environment. The polluted environment acts as a health hazard for the laborers. Thus, the social cost of production rises.

(b). Diseconomies of Strains on Infrastructure:

The localization of an industry puts excessive pressure on transportation facilities in the region. As a result of this, the transportation of raw materials and finished goods gets delayed. The communication system in the region is also overtaxed. As a result of the strains on infrastructure, monetary as well as the real costs of production rise.

(c). Diseconomies of High Factor Prices:

The excessive concentration of an industry in a particular industrial area leads to keener competition among the firms for the factors of production. As a result of this, the prices of the factors of production go up. Hence, the expansion and growth of industry would lead to a rise in costs of production.

Price

Economic price theory asserts that in a free market economy the market price reflects the interaction between supply and demand: the price is set to equate the quantity being supplied and that being demanded.

Meaning:

A **price** is the quantity of payment or compensation given by one party to another in return for one unit of goods or services. A price is influenced by both production costs and demand for the product. A price may be determined by a monopolist or may be imposed on the firm by market conditions.

Meaning of Pricing Policy:

A pricing policy is a standing answer to the recurring question. A systematic approach to pricing requires the decision that an individual pricing situation is generalized and codified into a policy coverage of all the principal pricing problems. Policies can and should be tailored to various competitive situations. A policy approach that is becoming normal for sales activities is comparatively rare in pricing.

Objectives of Pricing Policy:

The pricing policy of the firm may vary from firm to firm depending on its objective. In practice, we find many prices for a product of a firm such as wholesale price, retail price, published price, quoted price, actual price, and so on.

Following are pricing objectives:

(i) Price-Profit Satisfaction: The firms are interested in keeping their prices stable within a certain period of time irrespective of changes in demand and costs, so that they may get the expected profit.

(ii) Sales Maximisation and Growth: A firm has to set a price that assures maximum sales of the product. Firms set a price that would enhance the sale of the entire product line. It is only then, it can achieve growth.

(iii) Making Money: Some firms want to use their special position in the industry by selling products at a premium and make a quick profit as much as possible.

(iv) Preventing Competition: Unrestricted competition and lack of planning can result in wasteful duplication of resources. The price system in a competitive economy might not reflect society's real needs. By adopting a suitable price policy the firm can restrict the entry of rivals.

(v) Market Share: The firm wants to secure a large share in the market by following a suitable price policy. It wants to acquire a dominating leadership position in the market. Many managers believe that revenue maximization will lead to long-run profit maximization and market share growth.

(vi) Survival: In these days of severe competition and business uncertainties, the firm must set a price that would safeguard the welfare of the firm. A firm is always in its survival stage. For the sake of its continued existence, it must tolerate all kinds of obstacles and challenges from its rivals.

(vii) Market Penetration: Some companies want to maximize unit sales. They believe that a higher sales volume will lead to lower unit costs and higher long-run profit. They set the lowest price, assuming the market is price sensitive. This is called market penetration pricing.

(viii) Marketing Skimming: Many companies favor setting high prices to 'skim' the market. Dupont is a prime practitioner of market skimming pricing. With each innovation, it estimates the highest price it can charge given the comparative benefits of its new product versus the available substitutes.

(ix) Early Cash Recovery: Some firms set a price that will create a mad rush for the product and recover cash early. They may also set a low price as a caution against the uncertainty of the future.

(x) Satisfactory Rate of Return: Many companies try to set the price that will maximize current profits. To estimate the demand and costs associated with alternative prices, they choose the price that produces maximum current profit, cash flow, or rate of return on investment.

Methods of Pricing Methods

Introduction: An organization has various options for selecting a pricing method. Prices are based on three dimensions that are cost, demand, and competition. The organization can use any of the dimensions or a combination of dimensions to set the price of a product.

The figure shows different pricing methods:

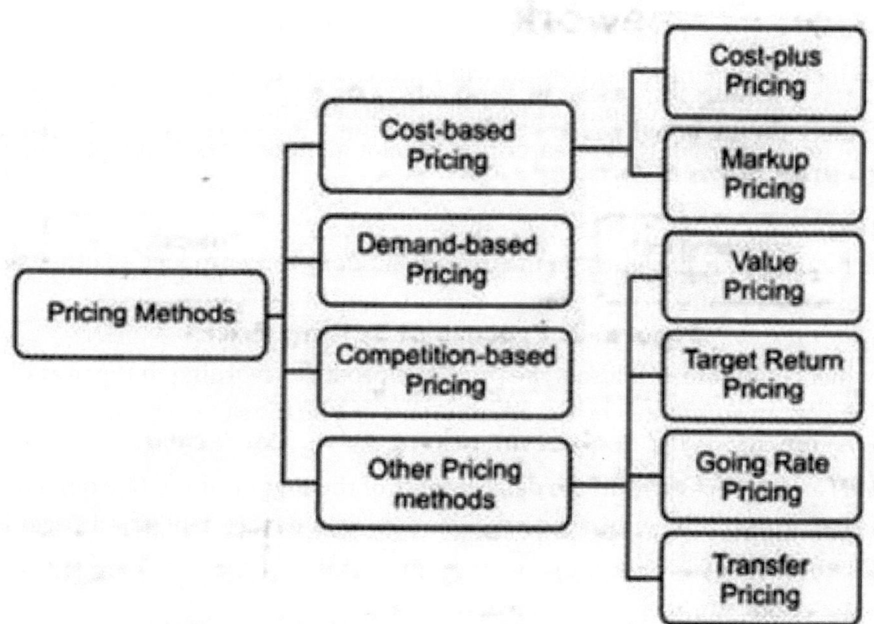

Fig: various pricing method

Cost-based Pricing:

Cost-based pricing refers to a pricing method in which some percentage of desired profit margins is added to the cost of the product to obtain the final price. In other words, cost-based pricing can be defined as a pricing method in which a certain percentage of the total cost of production is added to the cost of the product to determine its selling price. Cost-based pricing can be of two types, namely, cost-plus pricing and markup pricing.

These two types of cost-based pricing are as follows:

i. Cost-plus Pricing:

Refers to the simplest method of determining the price of a product. In the cost-plus pricing method, a fixed percentage, also called mark-up percentage, of the total cost (as a profit) is added to the total cost to set the price.

ii. Markup Pricing:

Refers to a pricing method in which the fixed amount or the percentage of the cost of the product is added to the product's price to get the selling price of the product. Markup pricing is more common in retailing in which a retailer sells the product to earn profit. For example, if a retailer has taken a product from the wholesaler for Rs. 100, then he/she might add up markup of Rs. 20 to gain profit.

Demand-based Pricing:

Demand-based pricing refers to a pricing method in which the price of a product is finalized according to its demand. If the demand for a product is more, an organization prefers to set high prices for products to gain profit; whereas, if the demand for a product is less, the low prices are charged to attract the customers.

Competition-based Pricing:

Competition-based pricing refers to a method in which an organization considers the prices of competitors' products to set the prices of its products. The organization may charge higher, lower, or equal prices as compared to the prices of its competitors.

Other Pricing Methods:

i. Value Pricing:

Implies a method in which an organization tries to win loyal customers by charging low prices for their high-quality products. The organization aims to become a low-cost producer without sacrificing quality. It can deliver high-quality products at low prices by improving its research and development process. Value pricing is also called value-optimized pricing.

ii. Target Return Pricing:

Helps in achieving the required rate of return on the investment done for a product. In other words, the price of a product is fixed based on expected profit.

iii. Going Rate Pricing:

Implies a method in which an organization sets the price of a product according to the prevailing price trends in the market. Thus, the pricing strategy adopted by the organization can be the same or similar to other organizations.

iv. Transfer Pricing:

Involves selling of goods and services within the departments of the organization. It is done to manage the profit and loss ratios of different departments within the organization. One department of an organization can sell its products to other departments at low prices.

Pricing over Product Life Cycle

Introduction: A Product's Life Cycle (PLC) can be divided into several stages characterized by the revenue generated by the product. The life cycle concept may apply to a brand or a category of product.

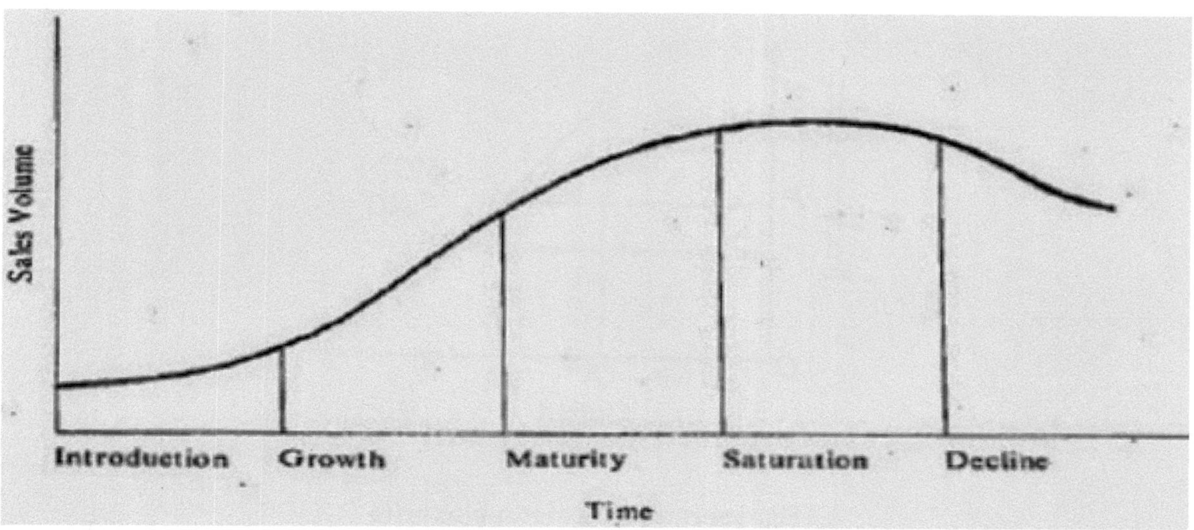

Fig: pricing over product life cycle

Introduction Stage:

When the product is introduced, sales will be low until customers become aware of the product and its benefits. Some firms may announce their product before it is introduced, but such announcements also alert competitors and remove the element of surprise.

Price under Introduction Stage:

Generally high, assuming a skim pricing strategy for a high-profit margin as the early adopters buy the product and the firm seeks to recoup development costs quickly.

Growth Stage:

The growth stage is a period of rapid revenue growth. Sales increase as more customers become aware of the product and its benefits and additional market segments are targeted.

Maturity Stage:

The maturity stage is the most profitable. While sales continue to increase in this stage, they do so at a slower pace. Because brand awareness is strong, advertising expenditures will be reduced.

Price under Maturity Stage:

Possible price reductions in response to competition while avoiding a price war.

Decline Stage:

Eventually, sales begin to decline as the market becomes saturated, the product becomes technologically obsolete, or customer tastes change. If the product has developed brand loyalty, the profitability may be maintained longer.

Price under Decline Stage:

Prices may be lowered to liquidate inventory of discontinued products. Prices may be maintained for continued products serving a niche market.

Cost-Plus Price: Determination, Advantages, and Criticisms

1. Determination of Cost-Plus Price 2. Advantages of Cost-Plus Price 3. Criticisms.

Determination of Cost-Plus Price:

Prof. Andrews in his study, Manufacturing Business, 1949, explains how a manufacturing firm fixes the selling price of its product based on the full-cost or average cost. The Andrews version of full-cost pricing is illustrated in Figure where AC is the average variable or direct costs curve which is shown as a horizontal straight line over a wide range of output. MC is its corresponding marginal cost curve. Suppose the firm chooses OQ level of output.

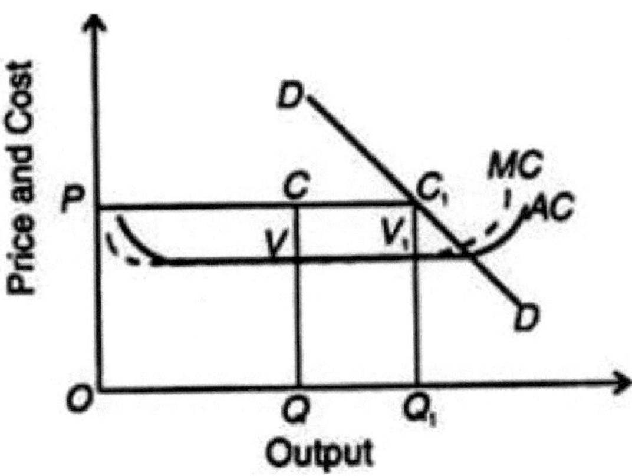

Fig: determination of cost-plus price

At this level of output, QC is the full cost of the firm made up of average direct cost QV plus the costing-margin VC. Its selling price OP will, therefore, equal QC.

The firm will continue to charge the same price OP but it might sell more depending upon the demand for its product, as represented by the curve DD. In this situation, it will sell OQ_1 output. **"This price will not be altered in response to changes in demand, but only in response to changes in the prices of the direct and indirect factors."**

Advantages of Cost-Plus Price:

The main advantages of cost-plus pricing are:

1. When costs are sufficiently stable for long periods, there is price stability which is both cheaper administratively and less irritating to retailers and customers.
2. The cost-plus formula is simple and easy to calculate.
3. The cost-plus method offers a guarantee against loss-making by a firm. If it finds that costs are rising, it can take appropriate steps by variations in output and price.
4. When the firm is unable to forecast the demand for its product, the cost-plus method can be used.
5. When it is not possible to gather market information for the product or it is expensive, cost-plus pricing is an appropriate method.
6. Cost-plus pricing is suitable in such cases where the nature and extent of competition are unpredictable.

Criticisms of Cost-Plus Price:

The cost-plus pricing theory has been criticized on the following grounds:

1. This method is based on costs and ignores the demand of the product which is an important variable in pricing.
2. It is not possible to accurately ascertain total costs in all cases.
3. This pricing method seems naive because it does not explicitly take into account the elasticity of demand. Where the price elasticity of demand of a product is low, the cost-plus price may be too low, and vice versa.
4. If fixed costs of a firm form a large proportion of its total cost, a circular relationship may arise in which the price would rise in a falling market and fall in an expanding market. This happens because the average fixed cost per unit of output is low when output is large and when output is small, the average fixed cost per unit of output is low.
5. Cost-plus pricing method is based on accounting data for total cost and not the opportunity cost that the sale of product incurs.

Conclusion

As you have observed, the cost-plus pricing method is one of the most basic methods of pricing and it is no surprise that it is also one of the more popular methods. However, it does have some major merits and demerits that you may have to consider before you select this approach.

Definition of 'Rate Of Return Pricing'

Definition: Rate of return pricing is a method by which a company fixes the price of the product in such a way that it ultimately helps organizations in achieving the ultimate goal or return on the capital employed. This is a common practice, but can only be effective in cases or products which have very little competition.

Description: The concept of rate of return pricing is similar to return on investment. The only difference is that in this approach, the manufacturer or the company can manipulate or change the price of the product to achieve the ultimate goal of the organization.

The rate of return pricing helps the company in achieving a certain level of profit which is required to keep the liquidity intact. The price is set in such a way that the ultimate goal of achieving corporate profit objective is met if sales continue to run at a given rate.

The process becomes easy if there is little competition, as compared to a situation when there is competition. The target return price can be defined as: Target return price = unit cost + (desired return * invested capital) / unit sales

Pricing the product by the rate of return can also have some shortcomings. It does not take into account the price elasticity and the pricing of the competition which are two important things to consider before the final pricing is set.

Let's understand the concept of rate of return pricing with the help of an example. A company ABC Ltd has an objective of achieving a required rate of return of say 20% on goods that they sell. The company manufactures pencils and has already invested Rs 10,00,000 in the business. The cost of each pencil is Rs 16. Here, we are assuming that sales can hit 50,000 units in a year.

The target return price would be = 16 (cost) + (20%*10,00,000 (investment))/50,000 (sales) = Rs 20. So, to achieve the required rate of return, the company should sell the pencil at Rs 20 each.

Revenue

The term revenue refers to the income obtained by a firm through the sale of goods at different prices. In the words of Dooley, 'the revenue of a firm is its sales, receipts or income'.

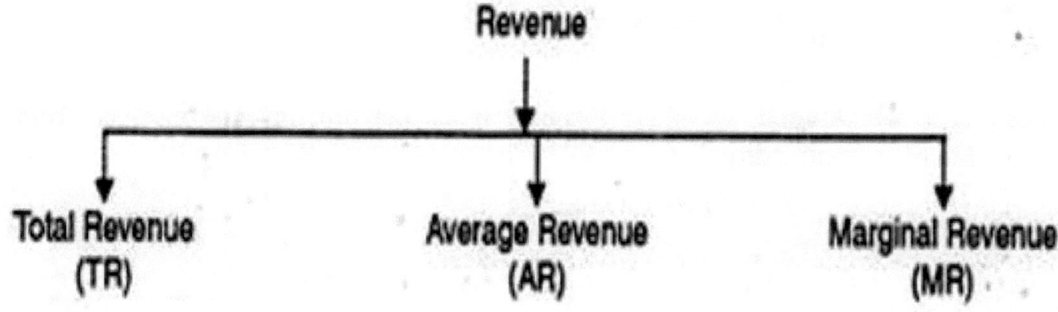

The revenue concepts are concerned with Total Revenue, Average Revenue, and Marginal Revenue.

1. Total Revenue:

The income earned by a seller or producer after selling the output is called the total revenue. Total revenue is the multiple of price and output. The behavior of total revenue depends on the market where the firm produces or sells.

"Total revenue is the sum of all sales, receipts or income of a firm." **Dooley**

Total revenue may be defined as the "product of planned sales (output) and expected selling price." **Clower and Due**

"Total revenue at any output is equal to the price per unit multiplied by the quantity sold." Stonier and Hague

Thus,

$$TR = AR \times Q$$

where

TR = Total Revenue

AR = Average Revenue or Price per Unit

Q = Output

For example if the price of a commodity is Rs. 100 and total units sold are 20 in that case total revenue will be

$$TR = 100 \times 20 = 200$$

$$TR = 2000$$

1.Average Revenue:

Average revenue refers to the revenue obtained by the seller by selling the per unit commodity. It is obtained by dividing the total revenue by total output.

"The average revenue curve shows that the price of the firm's product is the same at each level of output." **Stonier and Hague**

Thus :

$$AR = \frac{TR}{Q}$$

where

AR = Average Revenue

TR = Total Revenue

Q = Output

According to McDonnell, "Average Revenue is the per unit revenue received from the sale of one unit of a commodity."

$$TR = \text{Price} \times \text{Output}$$

$$TR = Pq$$

$$AR = \frac{Pq}{q} = P$$

and $P = f(Q)$ is an average curve which shows that price is a function of quantity demanded. It is also a demand curve.

3. Marginal Revenue:

Marginal revenue is the net revenue obtained by selling an additional unit of the commodity. "Marginal revenue is the change in total revenue which results from the sale of one more or one less unit of output." Ferguson. Thus, marginal revenue is the addition made to the total revenue by selling one more unit of the good. In algebraic terms, marginal revenue is the net addition to the total revenue by selling n units of a commodity instead of n – 1.

Therefore,

$$MR = \frac{\Delta TR}{\Delta Q}$$

$$MR_n = TR_n - TR_{n-1}$$

Whereas

TR_n = Total Revenue of 'n' units

TR_{n-1} = Total Revenue from (n – 1) units

$MR_{(nth)}$ = Marginal revenue from nth unit

n = Any given number

Koutsoyiannis, "The marginal revenue is the change in total revenue resulting from selling an additional unit of the commodity."

If total revenue from (n) units is 110 and from (n – 1) units is 100.

in that case

$$MR_{nth} = TR_n - TR_{n-1} = 100 - 100$$

$$MR_{nth} = 10$$

MR in mathematical terms is the ratio of change in total revenue to change in output

MR = ΔTR/Δq or dR/dq = MR

Total Revenue, Average Revenue, and Marginal Revenue:

The relation of total revenue, average revenue, and marginal revenue can be explained with the help of table and fig.

Table Representation:

The relationship between TR, AR, and MR can be expressed with the help of table .

Table 1

Unit (q)	TR/q AR or Price	(Pq) TR	($TR_n - TR_{n-1}$) MR
1	10	10	10
2	9	18	8
3	8	24	6
4	7	28	4
5	6	30	2
6	5	30	0
7	4	28	– 2
8	3	24	– 4
9	2	18	– 6
10	1	10	– 8

Table representation

From table we can draw the idea that as the price falls from Rs. 10 to Re. 1, the output sold increases from 1 to 10. Total revenue increases from 10 to 30, at 5 units. However, at the 6th unit, it becomes constant and ultimately starts falling at the next unit i.e. 7th. In the same way, when AR falls, MR falls more and becomes zero at the 6th unit and then negative. Therefore, it is clear that when AR falls, MR also falls more than that of AR: TR increases initially at a diminishing rate, it reaches the maximum and then starts falling.

The formula to calculate TR, AR and MR are as under:

$$TR = P \times Q$$

$$\text{Or } TR = MR_1 + MR_2 + MR_3 + MR_3 + \ldots.. MR_n$$

$$TR$$

$$AR = TR/q \quad MR = TR_n - TR_{n\,-\,x}$$

In fig. three concepts of revenue have been explained. The units of output have been shown on the horizontal axis while revenue on the vertical axis. Here TR, AR, MR are total revenue, average revenue, and marginal revenue curves respectively.

In figure , a total revenue curve is sloping upward from the origin to point K. From point K to K' total revenue is constant. But at point K' total revenue is maximum and begins to fall. It means even by selling more units total revenue is falling. In such a situation, marginal revenue becomes negative.

Similarly, in figure average revenue curves are sloping downward. It means average revenue falls as more and more units are sold.

In fig. MR is the marginal revenue curve that slopes downward. It signifies the fact that MR with the sale of every additional unit tends to diminish. Moreover, it is also clear from the fig. that when both AR and MR are falling, MR is less than AR. MR can be zero, positive or negative but AR is always positive.

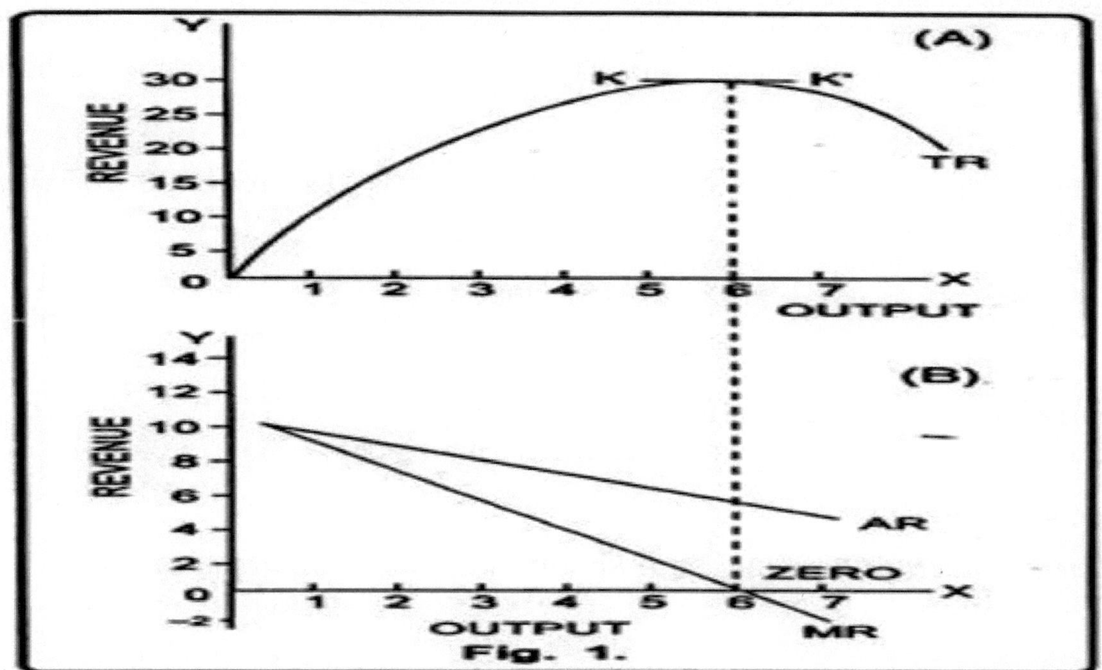

Fig: concepts of revenue

Total Revenue

A firm sells 100 units of a particular commodity for Rs. 10 each. If you were to calculate the amount realized by the firm, the answer is simple – Rs. 1,000 (100 x 10). This is the total revenue for the firm.

Hence, the total revenue refers to the amount of money realized by a firm on the sale of a commodity. Total revenue is expressed as follows:

TR = P x Q ... where TR – Total Revenue, P – Price, and Q – Quantity of the commodity sold.

Average Revenue

Average revenue is simply the revenue earned per unit of the output. In simpler words, it is the price of one unit of the output. Average revenue is expressed as follows:

Rs.Rs.AR = \frac {TR}{Q}Rs.Rs. ... where AR – Average Revenue, TR – Total Revenue, and Q – Quantity of the commodity sold.

By using the formula for total revenue, we get

Rs.Rs.AR = \frac {P × Q}{Q} Rs. Or AR = P

For example, a firm sells 100 units of a commodity and realizes a total revenue of Rs. 1,000. Therefore, its average revenue is Rs. AR = \frac {1000}{100}= Rs. 10Rs.Rs.

Hence, the firm sells the commodity at Rs. 10 per unit.

Marginal Revenue

Marginal revenue (MR) is the change in total revenue resulting from the sale of an additional unit of a commodity.

For example, consider a firm selling 100 units of a commodity and realizing a total revenue of Rs. 1,000. Further, it realizes a total revenue of Rs. 1,200 after selling 101 units of the same commodity.

Therefore, the marginal revenue is Rs. 200.

Marginal revenue is also defined as the rate of change of total revenue resulting from the sale of an additional unit of a commodity.

Therefore,

Rs.Rs.MR = \frac {ΔTR}{ΔQ}Rs.Rs. ... where MR – Marginal revenue, TR – Total revenue, Q – Quantity of the commodity sold, and Δ – the rate of change.

Further, for one unit change in output, we have

$$MR_n = TR_n - TR_{n-1}$$

Where,

- TR_n – the total revenue when the sales are at the rate of 'n' units per period.
- TR_{n-1} – the total revenue when the sales are at the rate of (n-1) units per period.

Marginal Revenue, Average Revenue, Total Revenue and the Elasticity of Demand

It is important to note that the marginal revenue, average revenue, and price elasticity of demand are related to one another through the following formula:

Rs.MR = AR×\frac {e – 1}{e}Rs.. ... where 'e' is the price elasticity of demand.

Further,

- If e = 1, then Rs.Rs.MR = AR×\frac {1 – 1}{1}= 0Rs.
- If e > 1, then MR is positive.
- If e < 1, then MR is negative.

For Example – The price is Rs. 20 and the quantity demanded is 15 units. Therefore, the total revenue is

TR_1 = Price x Quantity = 20 x 15 = Rs. 300.

Scenario 2 – Price is Rs. 18 and the quantity demanded is 16 units. Therefore, the total revenue is

TR_2 = Price x Quantity = 18 x 16 = Rs. 288.

From the definition of marginal revenue, we know that

$MR_n = TR_n - TR_{n-1}$

Therefore, we have

Marginal Revenue = $TR_2 - TR_1$ = 300 – 288 = Rs. 12.

Hence, the correct answer is option c – Rs. 12.

Product Pricing

CONCEPT OF FIRM AND INDUSTRY

In economics, a firm holds important position as at the firm level managerial decisions are taken. In common language a firm is considered as a manufacturing unit involved in production of goods. The scope of the term firm in economics is broad. It represents any business organization inhering service & agriculture organization also.

Definition of Firm

Some definitions of firm given by renowned economists are given below.

1. Firm is a unit of production that employs factors of production (or inputs) to produce goods & services under given state of technology.

2. It is an independently administered business unit – Hanson.

3. It is a center of control where the decisions about what to produce & how to produce are taken.

4. It is a business unit which hires productive resources for the purpose of producing goods & services.

5. A firm is an independent organization whose destiny is determined by the magnitude of the aggregate pay off & in which the aggregate pay off production & sale of goods or services (Harvey Leibenstein).

All these definitions have evolved during different time periods. They try to emphasis the different economic problems faced by firms. From various definitions different characteristic features of firm emerge which are listed below.

1. It is a place where all decision making related to production are taken *viz* what, where & how much to produce.

2. It is a place where manpower is hired for production.

3. It is a place where all the resources of production are brought together, production is done as well as sale & distribution of the manufactured product is carried out.

4. The state of technology is defined by the firms production function.

A firm is required to carry out all diverse functions related to production & marketing at the same time. While earning profit, firm as a production unit tries to manufacture the goods or provide service as per the consumer demand. The main objective of any firm is to maximize profit. Traditionally it was assumed that firm tries to maximize profit in each time period. But now it is realized that firm's objective should be to maximize profit in long run irrespective of profit or loss in short run.

Industry

Industry is a group of related firms. The relationship between the firms may be either based upon product or process criterion, e.g. dairy industry or food processing industry etc. The concept of industry is helpful to government and businessmen to formulate their policies.

Types of industry

The activities which are undertaken to produce, convert, extract and fabricate raw materials into finished goods are termed as industries. It is the process where goods are made usable and consumable. There are four different types of industries. These are:

a) Genetic Industry: It involves activities in reproducing and multiplying certain species of plants and animals for the sake of earning profit from their sale. Fish culture, cattle breeding, goatery and piggery are included in genetic industries.

b) Extractive Industry: The industries engaged with the discovery or extracting natural resources like minerals soil, water and forests are called extractive industries. Mining, agriculture and fishing are best examples of extractive industries.

c) Manufacturing Industries: The industries engaged in the conversion of raw material into finished products are called manufacturing industries. Cotton textile, sugar, iron and steel are the best examples of manufacturing industries.

d) Construction Industry: The industries in the construction of infrastructure like building, dams, roads, bridges and canals are called construction industries

Market structure is best defined as the organizational and other characteristics of a market. We focus on those characteristics which affect the nature of competition and pricing – but it is important not to place too much emphasis simply on the market share of the existing firms in an industry.

Meaning of Market structure: Market structure refers to the nature and degree of competition in the market for goods and services. The structures of market both for goods market and service (factor) market are determined by the nature of competition prevailing in a particular market.

Classification of market forms based on competition

Introduction: A market structure comprises several interrelated features or characteristics of a market. These features include the number of buyers and sellers in the market, level and type of competition, degree of differentiation in products, and entry and exit of organizations from the market.

Different types of market structures based on the competition

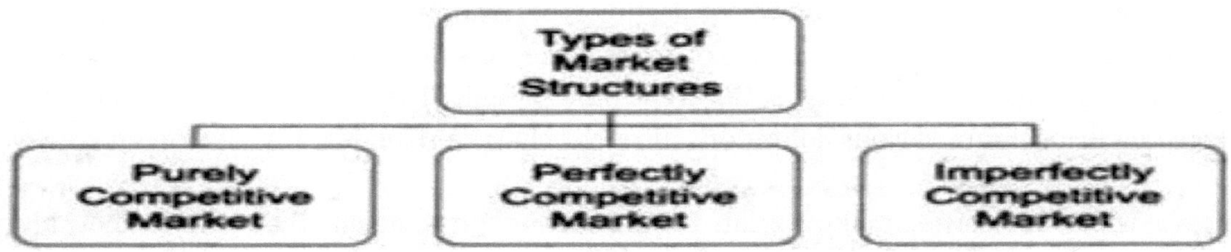

These different types of market structures

1. Purely Competitive Market:

A purely competitive market is one in which there are a large number of independent buyers and sellers dealing with standardized products. In pure competition, the products are standardized because they are either identical to each other or homogenous. Moreover, in pure competition, the average revenue curve or demand curve is represented by a horizontal straight line. This implies the homogeneity of products with a fixed market price.

The figure shows the average revenue curve under the pure competition curve:

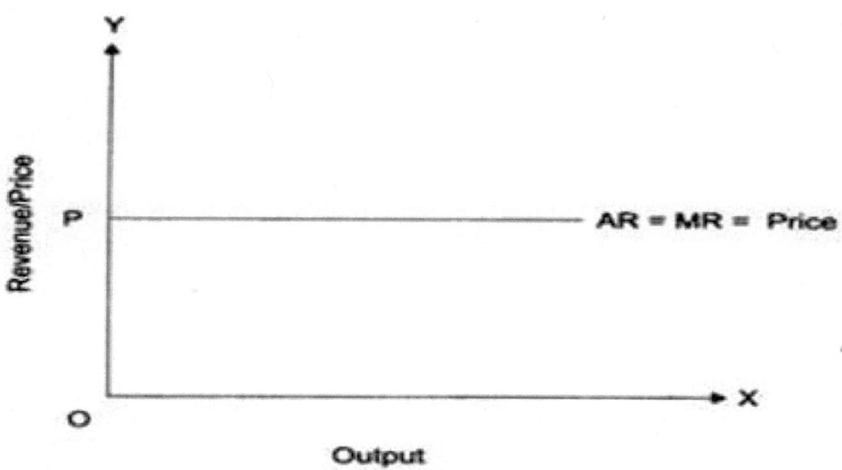

Fig: average revenue curve under pure competition curve

Figure OP is the price level at which a seller can sell any quantity of products at the fixed market price.

2. Perfectly Competitive Market:

In a purely competitive market, there are a large number of buyers and sellers dealing with homogenous products. A perfectly competitive market is a wider term than a purely competitive market. A perfectly competitive market is characterized by a situation when there is perfect competition in the market.

According to Bilas, "The perfect competition is characterized by the presence of many firms. They all sell identical products. The seller is a price taker, not a price maker."

3. Imperfectly Competitive Market:

In economic terms, imperfect competition is a market situation under which the conditions necessary for perfect competition are not satisfied. In other words, imperfect competition can be defined as a type of market that is free from the stringent rules of perfect competition.

Unlike perfect competition, imperfect competition is characterized by differentiated products. The concept of imperfect competition was firstly explained by an English economist, Joan Robinson.

The different forms of imperfect competition.

Monopoly:

The term monopoly has been derived from the Greek word Monopolian, which signifies a single seller. Monopoly refers to a market structure in which there is a single producer or seller that has control over the entire market. This single seller deals in products that have no close substitutes.

Monopolistic Competition:

The term monopolistic competition was given by **Prof Edward H. Chamberlin of Harvard University** in 1933 in his book Theory of Monopolistic Competition. We have discussed the concepts, perfect competition and monopoly. However, the real market situation is just the middle way between these two extreme market conditions.

Oligopoly:

The term oligopoly has been derived from two Greek words, oligoi means few and poly means control. Therefore, oligopoly refers to a market form in which few sellers are dealing either in homogenous or differentiated products. In India, the aviation and telecommunication industries are the perfect example of an oligopoly market form.

In the words of **Prof. George J. Stigler**, "Oligopoly is a market situation in which a firm determines its marketing policies based on the expected behavior of close competitors."

According to **Prof. Leftwitch**, "Oligopoly is a market situation in which there is a small number of sellers and activities of every seller are important for others."

Duopoly:

In a duopoly, there are two sellers, selling either a homogeneous product or a differentiated product. These two sellers between them enjoy a monopoly in the sale of the product produced by them.

Monopsony

This is a back-to-front monopoly. There are several producers and sellers, but just one buyer. Monopsony also refers to the job market – when one major company or organization is by far the largest employer in a town.

Oligopsony

When there are many sellers but very few buyers – like a monopsony, but with more than one buyer. In this market, the buyers call the shots – it is a buyer's market. Buyers can play off one supplier against another, thus significantly reducing their costs.

Features of a Perfect Market

A perfect market has the following conditions:

1. Free and Perfect Competition: In a perfect market, there are no checks either on the buyers or sellers. They are free to buy or to sell to any person. It means there are no monopolies.

2. Cheap and Efficient Transport and Communication: Uniform price for the commodity would not be possible if the changes in the prices are not quickly adjusted or the commodity cannot be quickly transported. Thus cheap and efficient means of transport and communication are must.

3. Wide Extent: Sometimes the wide market is regarded as the same thing as the perfect market. For a wide market, the commodity should have permanent and universal demand. The commodity should be portable. Means of transport and communication should be quick. There should be peace and security and an extensive division of labor.

4. Large number of firms: In this market, a product is produced and sold by a large number of firms. Since there is a large number of firms, therefore each firm is supplying only a small part of the total supply in the market, thus no one firm has any market power. It implies that no firm can influence the price of the product rather each must accept the price set by the forces of market demand and supply. The firms are price-takers instead of price-makers.

5. Large number of buyers: In a perfectly competitive market, there are large numbers of buyers each demanding a small part of the total market supply of the product. As a result, no single buyer is in a position to influence the market price determined by the forces of market demand and supply.

6. Homogeneous Product: In a perfectly competitive market, all the firms produce and supply identical products. It means that the products of all the firms are perfect substitutes for each other. As a result of this, the price elasticity of demand for a firm's product is infinite.

7. Free entry and exit: In a perfectly competitive market, there are no restrictions on the entry of new firms into the market or on the exit of existing firms from the market.

8. Perfect knowledge: In a perfectly competitive market, the firms and the buyers possess perfect information about the market. It implies that no buyer or firm is ignorant about the price prevailing in the market.

9. Perfect mobility of factors of production: In a perfectly competitive market, the factors of production are completely mobile leading to factor-price equalization throughout the market.

Price and Output Determination under Perfect Competition

Introduction

Perfect competition refers to a market situation where there are a large number of buyers and sellers dealing in homogenous products. Moreover, under perfect competition, there are no legal, social, or technological barriers to the entry or exit of organizations.

Equilibrium under Perfect Competition:

As discussed earlier, in perfect competition, the price of a product is determined at a point at which the demand and supply curves intersect each other. This point is known as the equilibrium point. At this point, the quantity demanded and supplied is called equilibrium quantity.

The figure shows the equilibrium under perfect competition:

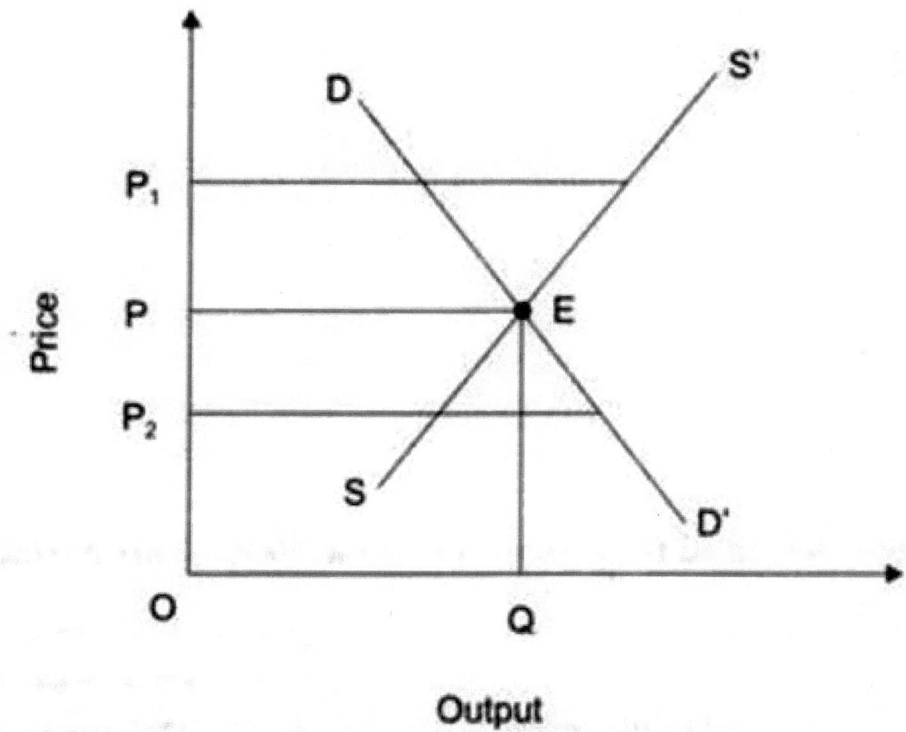

Fig: price and output determination under perfect compition

In Figure, it can be seen that at price OP1, supply is more than the demand. Therefore, prices will fall to OP. Similarly, at price OP2, demand is more than supply. Similarly, in such a case, the prices will rise to OP. Thus, E is the equilibrium at which equilibrium price is OP and equilibrium quantity is OQ.

Price determination under perfect competition can be analyzed into three periods:

i. Very Short Period: Refers to a time in which quantity supplied of a product cannot be increased with an increase in its demand.

ii. Short Period: Refers to a time in which the level of supply of a particular product can be increased, but only as per the production capacity of an organization. For example, an organization can produce 50 mobile phones in a day. This is the maximum production capacity of the organization.

iii. Long Period:

Refers to a period in which the supply of a product can be increased or decreased with the changing level of demand. In this period, organizations can install new machines or hire more labor to meet the supply requirements.

Price Determination in Very Short Period:

In a very short period, the total supply of a product is fixed. Every organization has a fixed stock of products to be sold thus supply curve IS perfectly inelastic in a very short time. Thus, the price of a product is influenced by demand.

The figure shows price determination in the very short period when demand influences the price:

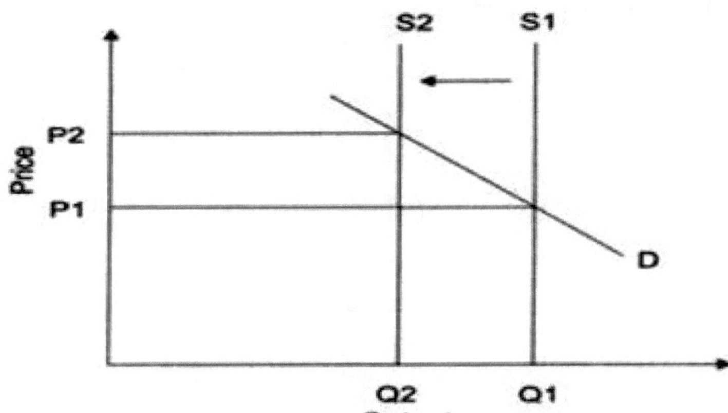

Fig: demand determined price in very short period

Now, suppose the demand for a product is fixed and its supply decreases due to various reasons, such as floods and an increase in prices of raw materials.

Price Determination in Short Period:

A short run refers to a period in which organizations do not change their scale of production. In this period, organizations neither exit the industry nor do new organizations enter the industry. In this period, it is possible to increase or decrease the supply of variable inputs. Thus, the supply curve is elastic.

The figure shows the price determination under the short run:

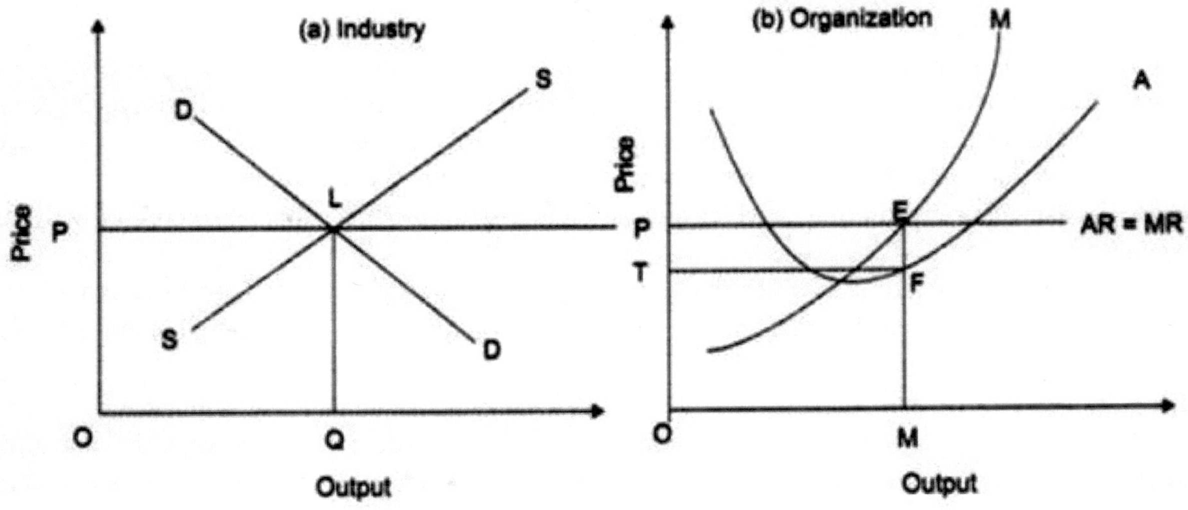

Fig: equlilbrium under short run

Generally, organizations have to select the level of output and price that maximizes their profits.

Equilibrium in Long Run:

The Ion. run refers to a period in which organizations can easily change variable and fixed factors, such as labor machinery and capital, ill the factors are variable in the long run. Organizations can expand the fixed equipment or can replace them. In addition, in this period, organizations can easily enter or exit the industry.

The long-run AC and MC curves are relevant for the price and output decisions. ATC is also an important determinant for equilibrium points in the long run. In a long time, the following two conditions must be satisfied for attaining equilibrium.

Price = MC

Price = AC

Or, Price = MC = AC

If price is greater than AC, organizations would make supernormal profits, which would influence new organizations to enter the industry. More organizations will increase the supply of the product and thus, the price of the product will fall. This will happen till the price reaches AC and all organizations are earning only normal profits.

On the other hand, if the price is below AC, organizations would incur losses. Organizations start exiting which leads to a fall in supply. This increases the price of AC. Thus, remaining organizations will start making normal profits.

It should be noted that when AC falls, MC is less than AC and when AC rises, MC is more than AC. Thus, MC=AC at the point where AC is neither falling nor rising is the minimum point of AC curve.

Thus, the equilibrium condition can be rewritten as:

Price = MC = Minimum of AC

The long-run equilibrium is shown with the help of Figure:

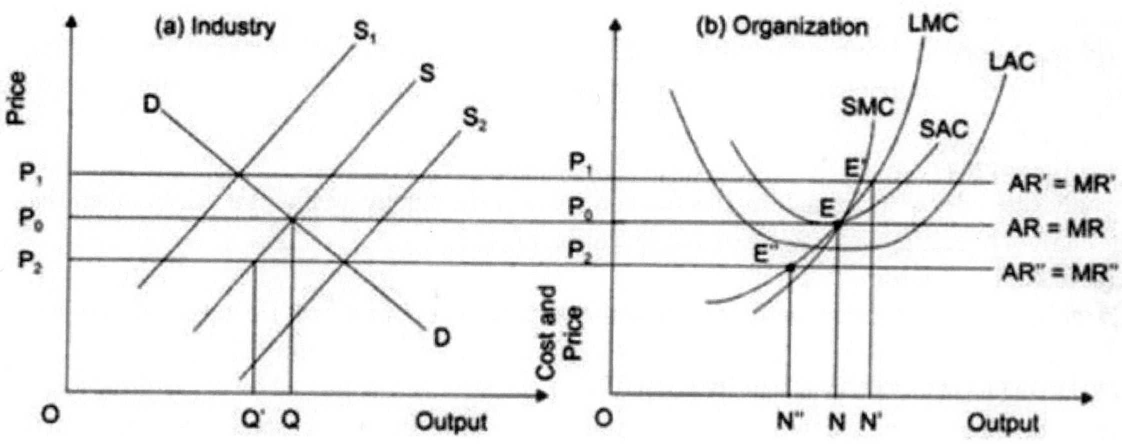

Fig: equilibrium in the long run

In long run, organizations can enter and exit the industry. In Figure, when the price is OP_1, equilibrium is achieved at point E'. At this point, AR is greater than AC, thus profits are gained. This lures other organizations to enter the industry. This will shift the supply curve of the industry from S_1 to S_2. Thus, the price will fall from OP_1 to OP_2.

Here, LMC=Price= minimum LAC. The conclusion that follows from the long-run equilibrium is that the competition forces organizations to produce at the minimum point of AC curve. This is beneficial for consumers as the product is produced at the cheapest possible cost.

Monopoly

Introduction: Monopolist has full control over the supply of the commodity. Having control over the supply of the commodity he possesses the market power to set the price. Thus, as a single seller, a monopolist may be a king without a crown. If there is to be a monopoly, the cross elasticity of demand between the product of the monopolist and the product of any other seller must be very small.

Meaning:

The word monopoly has been derived from the combination of two words i.e., 'Mono' and 'Poly'. Mono refers to a single and poly to control.

In this way, monopoly refers to a market situation in which there is only one seller of a commodity.

Definitions: "A pure monopoly exists when there is only one producer in the market. There are no dire competitions." –Ferguson

"Pure or absolute monopoly exists when a single firm is a sole producer for a product for which there are no close substitutes." –**McConnel**

Main Features of Monopoly Market

1. Single seller and a large number of buyers

A commodity or service is a **characteristic of the monopoly market.** Individual buyers cannot influence the price of the product.

2. No close substitute

Under a **Monopoly market**, the commodity or service sold by the seller has no close substitute.

3. One firm one industry

The seller or producer of a commodity or service is a firm as well as an industry. There is no distinction between the firm and industry under the Monopoly market.

4. Restriction on the entry

Under Monopoly, no form can enter the industry or market as there are several types of artificial and natural restrictions imposed by the monopolist this restriction may be in the form of copyright, patent, license, owner of mines, etc.

5. Control over the supply

Under Monopoly, the seller of a commodity has full control over the supply and he is a price maker. He is free to fix whatever the charges to attain his objective of maximization of profit.

6. Either price or supply fixation

A Monopoly either fixes the price or determines the supply of its product. He does not do both things simultaneously. To maximize his profit, he will either fix the price or control the supply of his output.

PRICE-OUTPUT DETERMINATION UNDER MONOPOLY:

A firm under monopoly faces a downward-sloping demand curve or average revenue curve. Further, in a monopoly, since average revenue falls as more units of output are sold, the marginal revenue is less than the average revenue. In other words, under monopoly, the MR curve lies below the AR curve.

The Equilibrium level in monopoly is that level of output in which marginal revenue equals marginal cost. The producer will continue producer as long as marginal revenue exceeds the marginal cost. At the point where MR is equal to MC the profit will be maximum and beyond this point, the producer will stop producing.

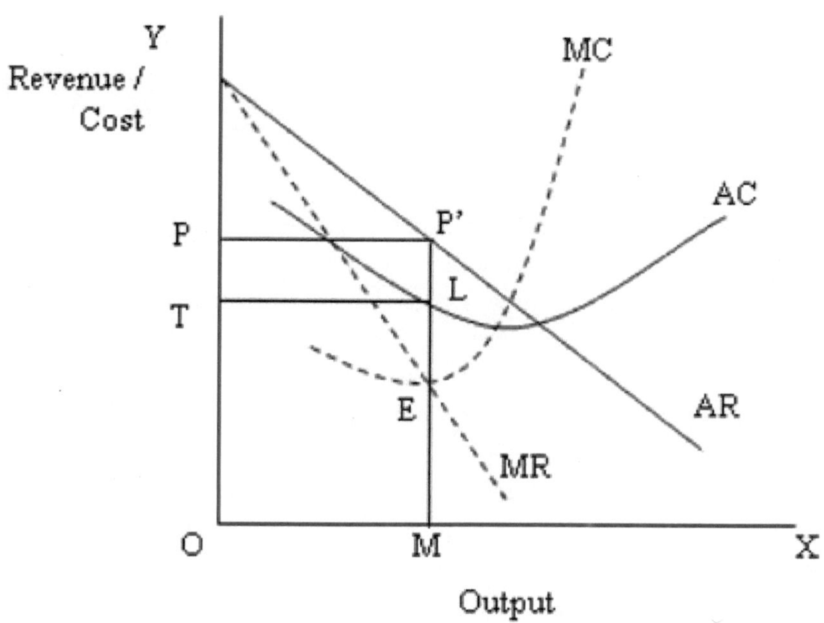

Fig: price-output determination under monoply

It can be seen from the diagram that up till OM output, marginal revenue is greater than marginal cost, but beyond OM the marginal revenue is less than marginal cost. Therefore, the monopolist will be in equilibrium at output OM where marginal revenue is equal to marginal cost and the profits are the greatest. The corresponding price in the diagram is MP' or OP. It can be seen from the diagram at output OM, while MP' is the average revenue, ML is the average cost, therefore, P'L is the profit per unit. Now the total profit is equal to P'L (profit per unit) multiply by OM (total output).

In the short run, the monopolist has to keep an eye on the variable cost, otherwise, he will stop producing. In the long run, the monopolist can change the size of the plant in response to a change in demand. In the long run, he will adjust the amount of the factors, fixed and variable, so that MR equals not only short-run MC but also long-run MC.

Monopolistic Competition

Definition: Under, **Monopolistic Competition**, there are a large number of firms that produce differentiated products which are close substitutes for each other. In other words, large sellers selling products that are similar, but not identical and compete with each other on other factors besides price.

Features of Monopolistic Competition

1. Free entry and exit of firms: Under this market structure, all the firms are free to enter and exit the industry as and where they are interested. New firms are free to enter the market with new brands of products that are close substitutes for the existing brands.

2. Product differentiation: Product differentiation is another characteristic of monopolistic competition. But these products are near substitute.

The differentiation is based on the quality, shape, size, packing, trademark, brand, color, the behavior of the seller, and location of the shop. However, being the differentiation the products of a seller are the close substitute of another seller.

3.A large number of buyers and sellers: In a monopolistic competition market, there is a large number of buyers and sellers. Sellers of a commodity or not in a position to affect the market behavior individually and the buyers purchase the goods as per their preferences.

The number of buyers and sellers is smaller than those of perfect competition in this market.

4. Non-price competition: Under monopolistic competition firms compete with one another without changing the prices of their products.

But they indulge in advertisement and sales promotion techniques (non-price competition) to attract more customers to boost their sales. Read Monopolistic competition reports.

5. Varying preferences of consumers: Under monopolistic competition, sellers are selling varied products which are different in quality and quantity. Buyers buy these products according to their preferences, income, etc. Buyers are attracted by the sellers based on the specialized qualities of their products.

6. Facilities for the customers: Under monopolistic competition sellers of a product provide various facilities to their customers so that they are attracted to purchase more of their products, credit facility, home delivery, repair facility. All these facilities attract customers.

7. The existence of competition and Monopoly elements: Under monopolistic competition, some of the characteristics of perfect competition are in existence such as a large number of buyers and sellers, free entry, and exit of firms in the industry.

8. The demand Curve is highly elastic: Under monopolistic competition, the demand curve is highly elastic because firms are free to enter and exit the industry.

Thus, we can say that product differentiation is the main character based on which monopolistic competition is recognized as a different market structure.

The price-output determination under Monopolistic Competition

The price-output determination under Monopolistic Competition: In monopolistic competition, since the product is differentiated between firms, each firm does not have a perfectly elastic demand for its products. In such a market, all firms determine the price of their products. Therefore, it faces a downward-sloping demand curve. Overall, we can say that the elasticity of demand increases as the differentiation between products decreases.

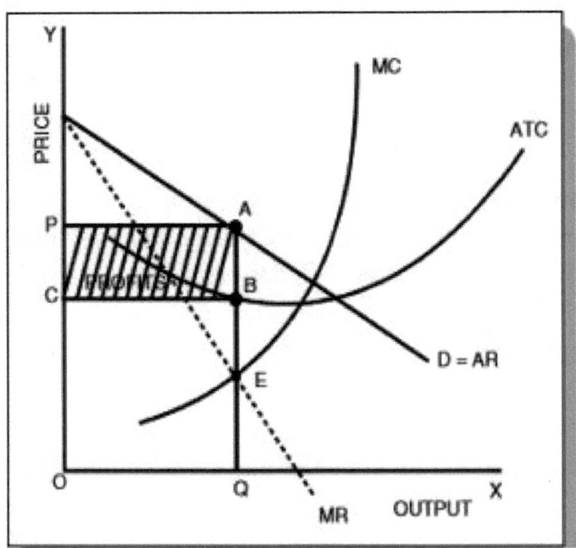

Fig: short run equilibrium of a firm in monopolistic competition: super normal profits

Fig. above depicts a firm facing a downward sloping, but flat demand curve. It also has a U-shaped short-run cost curve.

Conditions for the Equilibrium of an individual firm

The conditions for price-output determination and equilibrium of an individual firm are as follows:

1. MC = MR
2. The MC curve cuts the MR curve from below.

In Fig., we can see that the MC curve cuts the MR curve at point E. At this point,

- Equilibrium price = OP and
- Equilibrium output = OQ

Now, since the per-unit cost is BQ, we have

- Per unit super-normal profit (price-cost) = AB or PC.
- Total super-normal profit = APCB

The following figure depicts a firm earning losses in the short run.

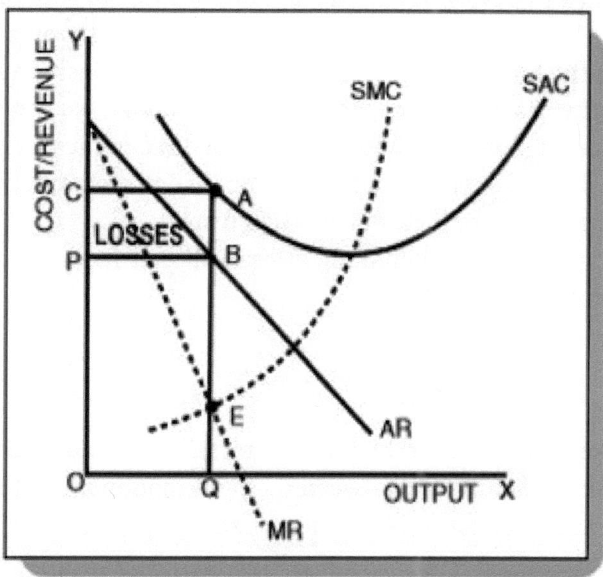

Fig:short run equlibrium of a firm in monopolistic competition- with losses

From Fig., we can see that the per-unit cost is higher than the price of the firm. Therefore,

- AQ > OP (or BQ)
- Loss per unit = AQ – BQ = AB
- Total losses = ACPB

Long-run equilibrium

If firms in a monopolistic competition earn super-normal profits in the short-run, then new firms will have an incentive to enter the industry. As these firms enter, the profits per firm decrease as the total demand gets shared between a larger number of firms. This continues until all firms earn only normal profits. Therefore, in the long run, firms, in such a market, earn only normal profits.

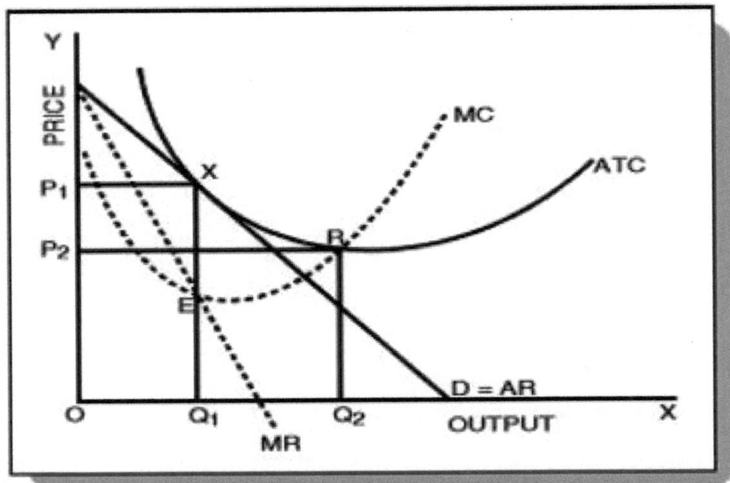

Fig: the long term equlibrium of the firm in a monopolistic competition

As we can see in Fig. above, the average revenue (AR) curve touches the average cost (ATC) curve at point X. This corresponds to quantity Q_1 and price P_1. Now, at equilibrium (MC = MR), all super-normal profits are zero since the average revenue = average costs. Therefore, all firms earn zero super-normal profits or earn only normal profits.

It is important to note that in the long run, a firm is in an equilibrium position having excess capacity. In simple words, it produces a lower quantity than its full capacity. From Fig. above, we can see that the firm can increase its output from Q_1 to Q_2 and reduce average costs. However, it does not do so because it reduces the average revenue more than the average costs. Hence, we can conclude that in monopolistic competition, firms do not operate optimally. There always exists an excess capacity of production with each firm.

In case of losses in the short-run, the firms making a loss will exit from the market. This continues until the remaining firms make normal profits only.

Oligopoly Market

Definition: The **Oligopoly Market** characterized by few sellers, selling homogeneous or differentiated products. In other words, the Oligopoly market structure lies between the pure monopoly and monopolistic competition, where few sellers dominate the market and have control over the price of the product.

Features of Oligopoly Market

1. **Interdependence:** The most important feature of Oligopoly is interdependence in the decision-making of the few firms which comprise the industry.

2. **Importance of Advertising and Selling Cost:** A direct effect of the interdependence of Oligopolists is that the various firms have to employ various aggressive and defensive marketing weapons to gain a greater share of the market or to maintain their share. For the various firms have to incur a good deal of the cost on advertising and other measures of sales promotion.

3. **Group Behaviour:** The theory of Oligopoly is a theory of Group behavior, not of mass or individual behavior, and to assume profit-maximizing behavior on the Oligopolists' part may not be very valid.

4. **A Small number of Sellers:** Oligopoly is a market in which there are few sellers of a commodity seller are selling a large part of the total supply of the commodity in the market and a seller is in a position to affect the price and activities of other firms.

5. Strong composition: Under this market condition, there is strong competition among various sellers. Each seller wants to retaliate its price based on the reaction of other sellers.

6. Homogeneous Product: Another important feature is Homogeneous products. When a producer is producing a Homogeneous product it is said to be a Homogeneous Oligopoly.

7. Heterogeneous Oligopoly: When a few sellers or producers are producing heterogeneous products or differentiated products it is said to be a heterogeneous Oligopoly.

8. Barriers to Entry of Firms: Barriers to entry to an Oligopolistic industry arise due to Huge investment requirement, Most advantage by the existing firm, Brand loyalty, Price cutting.

9. Lack of Uniformity: Another important feature is the Lack of uniformity. Size of the firms is not uniform. Some firms are very large while other firms are very small. This condition is called asymmetrical.

10. Price War: Oligopoly firms are always engaged in a price war. Product differentiation leads to the possibility of a price war. When any firm cut the price their firm's snail doing this same that results in the price war.

11. Demand Curve: Under the demand curve is indeterminate because of the mutual interdependence of the firms and actions or reactions of an individual firm affect other him as well.

5 Factor Market

Factor Market

"Factor market" is a term economists use for all of the resources that businesses use to purchase, rent, or hire what they need to produce goods or services. Those needs are the factors of production, which include raw materials, land, labour, and capital.

The factor market is also called the input market. By this definition, all markets are either factor markets, where businesses obtain the resources they need, or goods and services markets, where consumers make their purchases.

A factor market is termed an input market, while the market for finished products or services is an output market. This can be viewed as a closed-loop flow: In the factor market, households are sellers and businesses are buyers, while in the goods and services market, businesses are sellers and households are buyers.[1]

Workers are participating in the factor market when they make their services available to businesses. An individual member of a household who is looking for a job is participating in the factor market. An employee's wages are a component of the factor market, but the money will be spent in the goods and services market.

The factor market provides every component required to produce goods and services.

In the appliance manufacturing industry, workers who are skilled in refrigerator and dishwasher assembly are considered to be part of the factor market when they are available for hire. In the modern world, job search websites are part of the factor market.

Similarly, raw materials like steel and plastic—both of which are used to build refrigerators and dishwashers—are also examples of factor market products.

The Marginal Productivity Theory of Distribution

The marginal productivity theory of distribution, as developed by J. B. Clark, at the end of the 19th century, provides a general explanation of how the price (of the earnings) of a factor of production is determined.

In other words, it suggests some broad principles regarding the distribution of the national income among the four factors of production.

According to this theory, the price (or the earnings) of a factor tends to equal the value of its marginal product. Thus, rent is equal to the value of the marginal product (VMP) of land; wages are equal to the VMP of labour, and so on. Neo-classical economists have applied the same principle of profit maximization (MC = MR) to determine the factor price. Just as an entrepreneur maximises his total profits by equating MC and MR, he also maximises profits by equating the marginal product of each factor with its marginal cost.

Assumptions of the Theory:

The marginal productivity theory of distribution is based on the following seven assumptions:

1. **Perfect competition in both product and factor markets:**

Firstly, the theory assumes perfect competition in both product and factor markets. It means that both the price of the product and the price of the factor (say, labour) remains unchanged.

2.Operation of the law of diminishing returns:

Secondly, the theory assumes that the marginal product of a factor would diminish as additional units of the factor are employed while keeping other factors constant.

3.Homogeneity and divisibility of the factor:

Thirdly, all the units of a factor are assumed to be divisible and homogeneous. It means that a factor can be divided into small units and each unit of it will be of the same kind and the same quality.

4.Operation of the law of substitution:

Fourthly, the theory assumes the possibility of the substitution of different factors. It means that the factors like labour, capital, and others can be freely and easily substituted for one another. For example, land can be substituted by labour and labour by capital.

5.Profit maximisation:

Fifthly, the employer is assumed to employ the different factors in such a way and in such a proportion that he gets the maximum profits. This can be achieved by employing each factor up to that level at which the price of each is equal to the value of its marginal product.

6.Full employment of factors:

Sixthly, the theory assumes full employment for factors. Otherwise, each factor cannot be paid following its marginal product. If some units of a particular factor remain unemployed, they would be then willing to accept the employment at a price less than the value of their marginal product.:

7.Exhaustion of the total product:

Finally, the theory assumes that the payment to each factor according to its marginal productivity completely exhausts the total product, leaving neither a surplus nor a deficit at the end.

Some Key Concepts:

The theory is also based on key certain concepts.

These are the following:

- **MPP:**

The first is the marginal physical product of a factor. The marginal physical product (MPP) of a factor, say, of labour, is the increase in the total product of the firm as additional workers are employed by it.

- VMP:

The second concept is the value of the marginal product. If we multiply the MPP of a factor by the price of theproduct, we would get the value of the marginal product (VMP) of that factor.

- MRP:

The third concept is marginal revenue product (MRP). Under perfect competition, the VMP of the factor is equal to its marginal revenue product (MRP), which is the addition to the total revenue when more and more units of a factor are added to the fixed amount of other factors, or MRP = MPP x MR under perfect competition. It is simply

MPP multiplied by constant price, as P = MR. [VMP of a factor = MPP of the factor x price of the product per unit, and MRP of a factor=MPP of the factor x MR under perfect competition. So under perfect competition VMP of a factor = MRP of that factor.]

The Essence of the Theory:

The theory states that the firm employs each factor up to that number where its price is equal to its VMP. Thus, wages tend to be equal to the VMP of labour; interest is equal to VMP of capital, and so on. By equating VMP of each factor with its cost a profit-seeking firm maximises its total profits. Let us illustrate the theory concerning the determination of the price of labour, i.e., wages.

Let us suppose that the price of the product is Rs. 5 (constant) and the wages per unit of labour are Rs. 200 (constant). As the number of factors other than labour remains unchanged, wages represent the marginal cost (MC).

Table: Calculation of MPP, VMP, and MRP of a Variable Factor (Labour)

Land	Capital	Labour	Total Product	*MPP* of Labour	*VMP* or *MRP* of Labour	The Wage Rate *AW=MW*
1 unit	1 unit	1 unit	10 units	×	×	Rs. 20
"	"	2 units	16 "	6 units	Rs. 30	"
"	"	3 units	1 unit	5 units	Rs. 25	"
"	"	4 units	25 units	4 units	Rs. 20	"
"	"	5 units	28 "	3 units	Rs. 15	"
"	"	6 units	30 "	2 units	Rs. 10	"

Table represents calculation of MPP,VMP and MRP

Table shows that at 2 or 3 labourers, the VMP or MRP of labour is greater than wages; so the firm can earn more profits by employing additional labour. But at 5 or 6 labourers, the VMP or MRP of labour is less than wages, so it would reduce the number of labourers. But when it employs 4 labourers, the wage rate (Rs. 20) becomes

equal to the VMP or MRP of labour (also Rs. 20). Here the firm gets the maximum profits because its marginal cost of labour (or marginal wage Rs. 12) is equal to its marginal revenue (VMP or MRP, Rs. 20).

Thus, under the assumption of perfect competition a firm employs a factor up to that number at which the price of the factor is just equal to the value of the marginal product (=MRP of the factor). In the same way, it can be shown that rent is equal to the VMP of land, interest is equal to the VMP of capital, and so forth.

The theory may now be illustrated diagrammatically. See Fig. . Here WW is the wage line indicating the constant rate of wages at each level of employment (AW = MW. Here AW is average wage and MW is marginal wage). The VMP line shows the value of the marginal product curve of labour, and it goes downwards from left to right indicating diminishing MPP of labour. Fig. shows that the firm employs OL number of labourers, because by doing so it equates the MRP of labour with the wage ratio, and makes the optimum purchase of labour.

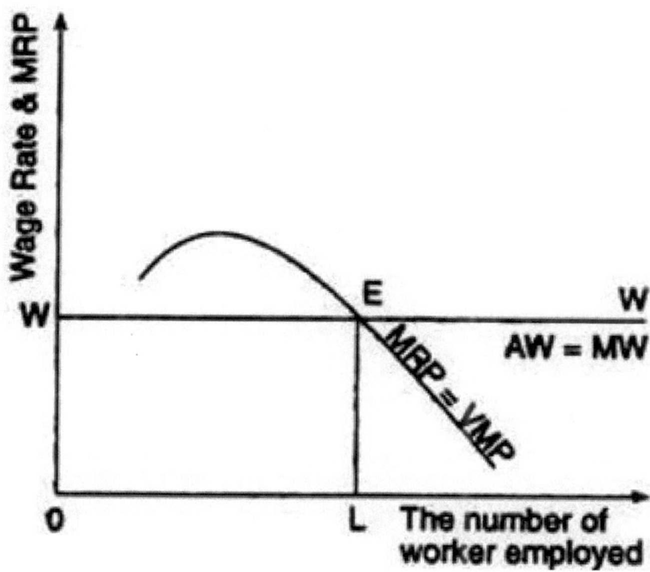

Fig: wage determination

Criticisms of the Theory:

The marginal productivity theory of distribution has been subjected to several criticisms:

- **In the determination of marginal product:**

Firstly, the main product is a joint product— produced by all the factors jointly. Hence the marginal product of any particular factor (say, land or labour) cannot be separately determined

- Unrealistic:

It is also shown that the employment of one additional unit of a factor may cause an improvement in the whole of the organisation in which case the MPP of the variable factors may increase. In such circumstances, if the factor is paid following the VMP, the total product will get exhausted before the distribution is completed. This is absurd. We cannot think of such a situation in reality.

- Market imperfection:

The theory assumes the existence of perfect competition, which is rarely found in the real world. But E. Chamberlin has shown that the theory can also be applied in the case of monopoly and imperfect competition, where the marginal price of a factor would be equal to its MRP (not to its VMP).

- Full employment:

Again, the assumption of full employment is also unrealistic. Full employment is also a myth, not a reflection of reality.

- Difficulties of factor substitution:

W. W. Leontief, the Nobel economist, denies the possibility of free substitution of the factors always owing to the technical conditions of production. In some products processes, one factor cannot be substituted by another. Moreover, organisation or entrepreneurship is a specific factor that cannot be substituted by any other factor.

- Emphasis on the demand side only:

The theory is one-sided as it ignores the supply side of a factor; it has emphasised only the demand side i.e., the employer's side, hi the opinion of Samuelson, the marginal productivity theory is simply a theory of one aspect of the demand for productive services by the firm.

- Inhuman theory:

Finally, the theory is often described as 'inhuman' as it treats human and non-human factors in the same way for the determination of factor prices.

RENT

Ricardian Theory of Rent (With Diagram)

The classical theory of rent is associated with the name of David Ricardo. He begins with a group of new settlers in a new country.

Let us suppose ourselves to be the settlers in a hitherto unknown island which we shall call Jawahar Island after our late beloved leader.

As we study the natural resources of Jawahar Island, we find the land to be of four grades. For convenience, we call them A, B, C, and D in the order of their fertility. We shall settle down in Tarapur in the 'A' part of the island

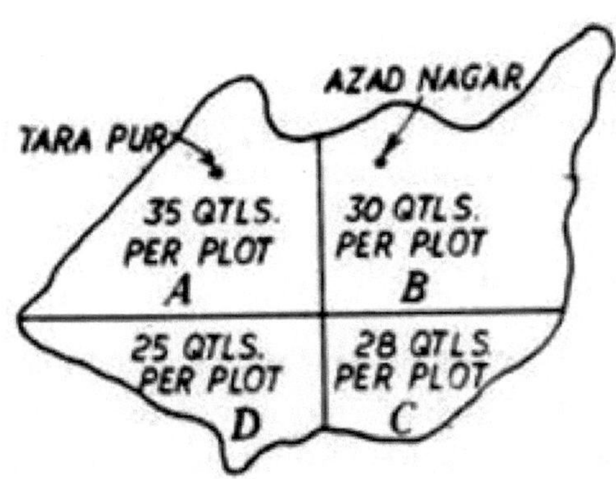

This is the most fertile land and gives us the largest produce per acre. Enough land is available of this quality to satisfy all our needs at the moment. Therefore, it is u free good and will not command any price, i.e., rent. But as time passes, the mouths to be fed increase in number. This may be due to more immigrants, who have heard of our good luck, or due to an increase in population.

Rent in Extensive Cultivation:

A time comes when all land of the best quality has been taken up. But some demand remains unsatisfied. We have then to resort to 'B' quality land. It is inferior to 'A' and yields only 30 quintals of wheat per plot as compared with 35 quintals of 'A' with the same expenditure of labour and capital. Naturally, plots in 'A' now acquire a greater value as compared with 'B'. A tenant will be prepared to pay up to 5 quintals of wheat to get a plot in the 'A' zone or take 'B' quality land free of charge.

This difference, paid to the owner (if the cultivator is a tenant) or kept to himself (if he is the owner), is economic rent. In the first case (i.e., when the cultivator is a tenant) it is contractual rent; and in the latter (i.e., when the cultivator is the owner) it is known as implicit rent. 'B' plots do not pay any rent. To go a step further, we see that after all land of 'B' quality has also been taken up, we begin cultivating 'C' plots. Now even 'B' quality land comes to have a differential surplus over 'C'. Rent of 'A' increases still further.

When the demand increases still more, we are pushed to the use of the worst land, which is of 'D' quality yielding 25 quintals per plot. 'D' quality land is now no-rent land or marginal land while 'A', 'B', 'C all earn rent. This growing demand shows itself in rising prices. They raise high enough to cover the expenses of cultivation on the lowest grade land, i.e., 'D' quality.

Let us suppose that one unit of productive effort is equal to Rs. 3,500. When only A' quality land, where a plot produces 35 quintals is under the plow, the price of wheat will be Rs. 100 per quintal. When owing to increased demand, the price of wheat rises to Rs.-110 then and only then will 'B' quality land be cultivated which produces 30 quintals of wheat. And when that happens 'A' land will have a surplus of 5 quintals X Rs. 110 = Rs. 550 per plot. This becomes rent.

The difference, in other words, between the return from a plot of land above the margin and the marginal plot (i.e., the one just paying its way) is called rent or economic rent.

Rent in Intensive Cultivation:

The settlers in Jawahar Island realize that there is another way too of increasing the productivity. Why not apply more labour and capital to superior lands, and resort to intensive cultivation? This is done but it is seen that the law of diminishing returns sets in. Look at Fig. 33.1 again. Now consider that A, B, C, and D are the different doses of labour and capital (instead of different grades of land) applied to the same grade of land. The first dose yields 35 quintals.

The second unit of labour and capital used on 'A' plot will almost definitely give us less than the first. We suppose it gives us only 30 quintals. So we have the choice of either taking new plots in 'B' land or cultivating 'A' lands more intensively. If we adopt the latter course, the first unit of labour and capital will be yielding a surplus over the second unit—which unit produces just enough to cover the expenses. This surplus, again, is rent. As more and more units of labour and capital are applied, the return per unit will go on falling.

Rent Due to Differential Advantages:

With time, however, a new factor emerges. A locality in the A' zone—marked Tarapur in Fig. 33.1—develops into a market and Azadnagar in 'B' into a railway junction, and produce has to be sent to those two flourishing localities for their final disposal. Now the plots situated in the neighborhood of Tarapur and Azadnagar come to have an advantage. They have either no transport charges or much smaller charges than in the case of lands in 'C' and D' areas.

Transport charges are a part of the cost of production because production is complete only when the commodity reaches the hands of consumers. The better-situated plots, which have to bear fewer transport charges, will enjoy a surplus over the distant ones. This surplus will be another cause of rent. Hence, economic rent is a surplus that arises on account of natural differential advantages, whether of fertility or situation, possessed by the land in question over the marginal land.

No-rent or Marginal Land:

The cases described above show that rent is earned due to certain pace being better suited for cultivation or being better situated regarding markets. But better than what? Of course better than some other plot of land. This 'some other' plot is marginal land which just covers its expenses and no more. This land is called 'no-rent land'. All rents are measured from it upwards.

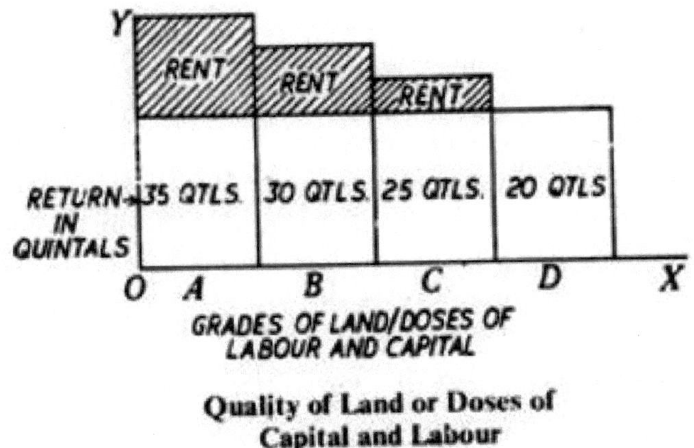

Quality of Land or Doses of Capital and Labour

In fig. 'D' quality and land which produces 20 quintals per plot is the marginal land. Here the return and cost are equal. It is just worthwhile cultivating this land since it just covers expenses of cultivation and yields no surplus to the cultivator.

It is quite possible that we may not be able to spot the 'no-rent land' because:

(a) It may be paying scarcity rent, or

(b) The owner might have invested some capital in it and the interest thereon might be mistaken for rent, or

(c) The no-rent land may be in some other country or

Scarcity Rent:

In our new home country, Jawahar Island, we, ,at last,, come to a situation when all the lands have been brought under thplow, and are being cultivated intensively too. But the price rises still further under the pressure of demand. The population has been increasing fast. Our country has become old and no more land is available as we are an island country. Prices of agricultural products go up and, therefore, incomes from land go up.

Hence, all land (including the no-rent 'D' quality land) begins to get surplus above expenses. This surplus above costs in the 'D' quality land, our previous no-rent land, is scarcity rent. Superior lands will be paying this surplus over and above differential gain.

Criticism of Ricardian Theory:

The Ricardian theory of rent has been widely criticized as under:

(i) It is pointed out that fertility of the land is not original:

Much of the present productive capacity of the land is the result of human efforts, use of manures, and other improvements. Thus, it is not possible to say which qualities of land are original and which of them are man's creations.

The situation is something that man cannot change. Obviously, it is not possible to move a plot of land to another place. But man can improve the means of transport so much that the distance between two places matters little Thus he can manage to change the character of a place. The planned cities and factory towns of today are the product of man's brain. Although this criticism has a leg to stand upon, it cannot be denied that certain original qualities do matter. No human effort will change Rajasthan into Kashmir.

(ii) The idea of indestructibility is objected to:

Area, it is said, is everlasting but not fertility. Continued cultivation exhausts fertility. We observe this in the case of land in India. Lands are reported to be less fertile and, therefore, less productive per hectare today than they were in the past.

Ricardo's doctrine, however, cannot be wholly rejected. Naturally fertile land regains its fertile qualities more easily if it is manured or left fallow. The creation of fertility in a barren land is more difficult. Besides no amount of use will entirely kill the fertility of the land.

(iii) Certain American economists like Carey have criticised the classical theory of rent on historical grounds. They say that cultivation did not begin with the most fertile lands when the first settlers arrived in America, nor did it pass on to the less fertile lands in that order. The reason was that some of the most fertile lands were covered with thick forests while others were open to enemy attack. The settlers naturally preferred less fertile areas which were open and could be defended.

This criticism answers itself. Not necessarily the most fertile, but the land offering the best reward for a definite effort is occupied first. Moreover, the order of cultivation is not so important. Even if the order is changed, when two types of land are being cultivated, the more fertile or better-situated plot will produce a surplus above the cost.

The surplus will arise whichever land is cultivated before the other. Rent will still arise even if all the lands were of uniform quality. It will arise in the intensive form.

(iv) It is said that rent is not due to differential advantages only. Even if all lands were of uniform quality, rent would still arise. Rent arises from scarcity.

(vi) The concept of marginal land is said to be imaginary, theoretical, and not realistic.

(vii) It is also urged that no special theory of rent is necessary. Demand and supply theory, which explains all values, can explain rent also.

(viii) Modern economists think that it is only from the point of view of the economy as a whole that land has a perfectly inelastic supply and earns a surplus or rent. This surplus is not included in the cost and hence does not enter into price. But from the point of view of individual farmers or industries, a payment has to be made to prevent the land from being transferred to some other use.

The payment, called transfer earnings, is an element of cost and hence enters into the price. For the individual farmer, the whole of rent is cost. "This concept of transfer earnings helps to bring the simple Ricardian Theory—where transfer earnings are zero because it is the whole economy which is being studied—into a closer relationship with reality."— (Stonier and Hague).

Rent as Payment for the Use of Land: Modern View:

So far as the use of land is concerned, modern economists have offered a better explanation of rent. This payment is determined by the demand for and the supply of land.

Demand Side:

The demand for land is a derived demand. It is derived from the demand for the products of the land. If the demand for these products rises or falls, the demand for the use of land will correspondingly rise or fall leading to an increase or decrease in rents. For instance, if the population of a country increases, the demand for food will increase, resulting in increased demand for land and a rise m its rent, and vice versa.

The demand for a factor of production depends on its marginal revenue productivity (or in short, marginal productivity). This productivity is subject to the law of diminishing marginal productivity. That is why, as in the case of other factors, the demand curve DD shown in the following figures slopes down from the left to the right. Thus, on the side of demand, the rent of land is determined by its productivity, not total productivity, but marginal productivity.

Supply Side:

The supply of land is fixed so far as the community is concerned, although individuals can increase their supply by acquiring more land from others or decrease its supply by parting with the land. Despite reclamation projects, the effect of which on the total supply is negligible, the supply of land remains practically fixed.

It is a case of perfectly inelastic supply, which means that whatever the rent (the rent may rise or fall), the supply remains the same. That is why it is said that land has no supply price. In other words, the supply of land, in general, is inelastic, and as such its supply is independent of what it earns.

Interaction of Demand and Supply:

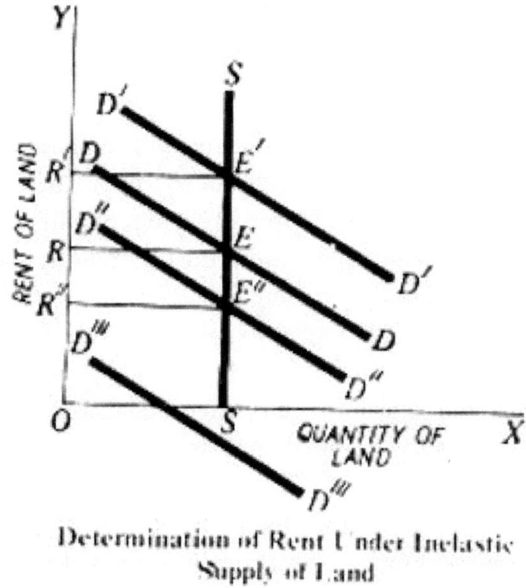

Determination of Rent Under Inelastic Supply of Land

Fig: interaction of demand and supply

We have analysed the demand and the supply sides of land. The interaction of these forces is shown in Fig. We assume that land is homogeneous and it is used for raising one crop only. Then there can be one demand curve and one supply curve. We also assume perfect competition. SS supply curve, a vertical straight line, represents fixed supply. We start with DD as the total demand curve for land. These two curves intersect at E.

In this position OR (=SE) is the rent. If rent is less (i.e., OR) the demand for land will increase; but the supply is fixed, hence rent will again rise to OR. Suppose rent rises above OR (i.e., to OR'), then the demand for land will decrease and bring the rent back to OR.

Suppose now that, on account of increase in population or otherwise, the demand for land has increased from DD to D'D'. The supply curve is still the same SS. The new point of intersection will be E' and therefore the rent will be OR'. If demand falls to D"D", the demand and supply curves intersect at E", and the rent will be OR". If the country is entirely new and land of good quality is surplus, then there will be no rent. The condition is shown by D' "D".

If the land is of different qualities, then each quality will have a separate demand curve and they will command different rents. Hence the theory explains differential rent too. Thus, the rent of land, like the remuneration of other factors, is determined by the equilibrium between demand for and supply of land.

In other words, it is scarcity in relation to demand that determines rent. Fundamentally speaking, rent is paid for land because the produce of land is scarce in relation to its demand. The scarcity of land is in fact derived from the scarcity of its products. It is this scarcity which explains all values and rent is no exception.

Land for a Particular Use:

We have analysed above total demand and total supply of land for the community as a whole. Let us now consider it from the point of view of a particular industry or use. For a particular use or industry, the supply of land cannot be regarded as fixed. By offering more rent, it can be increased; the supply will decrease if the rent in this particular case goes down.

The supply is thus elastic and the supply curve will rise upwards from left to right, as is shown in Fig. DD is the demand curve to start with. E is the point of intersection, hence OR (= EM) is the rent and OM is the land used.

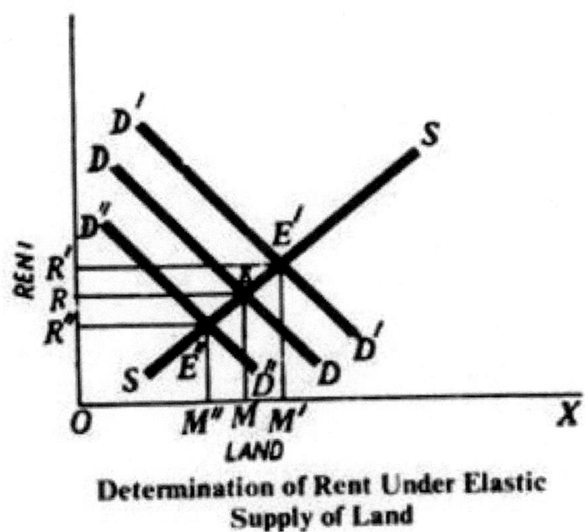

Determination of Rent Under Elastic Supply of Land

Fig: determination of real under elastic supply of land

Suppose demand increases to D'D'. Now the two curve? Intersect at E' and the rent will be OR' and the land used OM'. This means that since for this particular use, the rent of land has gone up, MM' land has been withdrawn from other uses and put to this use. Similarly, if demand decreases to D"D", the rent will come down to OR" and the quantity of land used to OM", which means MM" land has gone out of this particular use, sine: the rent has fallen.

QUASI-RENT

The concept of quasi-rent was introduced in economic theory by Marshall Marshall's concept of quasi-rent is the extension of the Ricardian concept of rent to the short-run earnings of the capital equipment (such as machinery, buildings etc.) which are in inelastic supply in the short run. The distinguishing characteristic of land is the fact that its supply is perfectly inelastic to changes in its price and therefore its earnings depend mainly upon the demand for it. But, in the short run, the fixed capital equipment such as machinery is likewise perfectly inelastic in supply and cost of its production is not relevant once it has been produced. During the short period, the earnings of specialized capital equipment depend mainly upon the demand conditions and are thus similar to land rent and have therefore been called rent by Marshall Since the capital equipment is not permanently in fixed supply like land and instead their supply is very much elastic in the long run, Marshall preferred to call their earnings in the short period as quasi-rent rather than rent.

The quasi-rent is only a temporary surplus which is enjoyed by the owner of the capital equipment in the short run due to the increase in demand for it and which will disappear in the long run due to the increase in the supply of capital equipment in response to the increased demand. In the short run, specialized machinery has no alternative use and therefore its supply will remain fixed in the i short run even if its earnings fall to zero. Thus, the transfer earnings of the capital equipment or machinery in the short run are zero. Therefore, the whole of the earnings of the machinery in the t short run are surplus over transfer earnings and therefore represent rent It may, however, be pointed out that some maintenance costs are required to be incurred in the short run to keep the machinery in the running order. Therefore, more precisely, the quasi-rent may be defined as the short-run earnings of a machine minus the short-run cost of keeping it in running order"

There is every reason to believe that quasi rent will be generally earned in the short run by thecapital equipment like machinery... buildings etc This is because, however keen competitionbetween entrepreneurs may be, the supply of capital equipment cannot be increased in the short tuh. Consequently, when very high earnings are being made from capital equipment they will not be competed away in the short run. But in the long run the position regarding the supply of capital equipment (e g., machines) is quite different Capital equipment are man-made instruments of production and therefore their supply can be increased in the long run to meet the increased demand for them.

Thus, as a result of the increase in the supply of machines, their excessive earnings will be competed away. In the long run, therefore, the competitive equilibrium is reached when the earnings from the capital equipment are just sufficient to maintain them in running order and provide only normal profits to entrepreneur. Thus, in the long run no surplus over cost of production is earned by the machines. Therefore, quasi-rent will disappear in the long-run competitive equilibrium Professors Stonier and Hague rightly remark, "The supply of machines is fixed in the short run whether they are paid much money or little so they earn a kind of rent. In the long run this rent disappears for it is not a true rent, but only an ephemeral reward-a 'quasi-rent.

Quasi-Rent- Total Revenue Earned - Total Variable Costs

Wage Differentials

Wage differentials bear a direct relationship to the diversity in occupation and industries that exist in the economic sphere of activity in a country. A certain job requiring a certain skill is paid more or less than another job requiring a different skill either in the same or some other industry. There are a variety of contributory factors.

There is a need to understand the reasons for these differences as in many cases there is a constant adjustment taking place in order to maintain the existing disparity, for instance, between the skilled and unskilled or semiskilled workers; between the officers and the supervisory or clerical staff and so on.

When there is a variation in workers' skills, i.e., highly skilled, skilled, semi-skilled and unskilled, their wage rates will differ. The variance is due to the complexity of the skill acquired, its scarcity, and the time taken in training to acquire it. The unskilled category which requires none of these is relatively less well paid.

There are certain jobs which involve physically heavy work, others which are strenuous but may not require very high degree of other skills, and yet again, there are certain jobs which require the workmen to work in unpleasant and dangerous conditions, like coal, miners, who have to work underground with poor ventilation and safety hazards. Yet they may not get high rates.

The economic factors or abundance of such workers may alter their bargaining strength. When the coal industry was replaced by oil, because of its lack of modernization, the wages of the coal-miners were depressed. Two factors need to be taken into account, the demand and supply for a particular category of skills and the state of prosperity of an industry or unit.

If it is depressed, this will have some effect on wages and consequently on the grades. The rate of dearness allowance (DA) depending on the index chosen will affect wage differentials. In many situations, arbitration or judicial pronouncements have favored a higher quantum for the lowest category of workers.

On a wide scale, there has not been a systematic attempt at job evaluation – an exercise which would have identified the differences in terms of skill training experience, etc. between jobs and provided for relative weightages which could lead to standardization and eradication of distinctions for the same type of jobs.

In the modern organized sector, where collective bargaining is prevalent, there is a trend towards job evaluation schemes. The influence of collective bargaining in terms of pushing up wages in some industries and regions has been quite significant, especially in situations where collective bargaining is coupled with union strength.

Finally, the difference in terms of a unit's level of productivity and profitability and its influence differentials has to be considered. If both productivity and profitability are high, then the wages sought and given are correspondingly bound to be high.

Salary Differentials and Economy Functions:

Salary differentials perform important economic, functions like labour productivity, attracting the people to different jobs. Since most of the workers are mobile with a view to maximising their earnings, wage differentials reflect in variations in productivity, efficiency of management, maximum utilisation of human force etc.

Attracting efficient workers, maximisation of employee commitment, development of skills, knowledge, utilisation of human resources, maximisation of productivity can be fulfilled through wage differentials, as the latter determines the direct allocation of manpower among different units, occupations and regions so that national production can be maximised. Thus, wage differentials provide an incentive for better allocation of human force, labour mobility among different regions and the like.

Salary differentials play pivotal role in a planned economy in the regulation of wages and development of national wage policy by allocating the skilled human force on priority basis. Development of new skills, knowledge etc., is an essential part of human resource development.

Shortage of technical and skilled personnel is not only a problem for industries but it creates bottlenecks, in the attainment of planned goals. Thus, wage differentials to certain extent, are desirable from the view point of national interest. As such, they probably become an essential part of national wage policy. Complete uniform national wage policy is impracticable and undesirable.

Wage Differentials – Concept and Definition

In this era of modern industrial organizations, wage differentials that show the differences in the rate of wages among workers working in the same unit, different units, different occupations, different regions and the like have emerged as a common feature of labour markets in various countries.

Wage differential refers to differences in wage rates due to the location of company, hours of work, working conditions, type of product manufactured, or other factors. It may be the difference in wages between workers with different skills working in the same industry or workers with similar skills working in different industries or regions.

We will get different terms as occupational wage differentials, inter-industry, inter-firm, inter-area or geographical differentials and personal differentials because wages differ in different employments or occupations, different industries and localities, and even between the persons in the same employment or grade, etc.

Wage differentials have been classified into three categories:

i. First, the differentials that can be attributed to imperfections in the employment markets, such as the limited knowledge of workers in regard to alternative job opportunities available elsewhere; obstacles to geographical, occupational or inter-firm mobility of workers; or time-lags in the adjustment of resource distribution and changes in the scope and structure of economic activities. Examples of such wage differentials are inter-industry, inter-firm, and geographical or inter- area wage differentials.

ii. Second, the wage differentials which originate in social values and prejudices and which are deeper and more persistent than economic factors. Wage differentials by sex, age, status or ethnic origin belong to this category.

iii. Third, occupational wage differentials, which would exist even if employment markets were perfect and social prejudices were absent.

Type # 1. Occupational Differentials:

These indicate that since different occupations require different qualifications, different wages of skill and carry different degrees of responsibility, wages are usually fixed on the basis of the differences in occupations and various degrees of skills.

The basic functions of such differentials are:

(a) To induce workers to undertake "more demanding", "more agreeable or dangerous" jobs, or those involving "a great chance of unemployment, or wide uncertainty of earnings."

(b) To provide an incentive to young person to incur the costs of training and education and encourage workers to develop skills in anticipation of higher earnings in future.

(c) To perform a social function by way of determining the social status of workers.

In countries adopting a course of planned economic development, skill differentials play an important role in manpower and employment programmes, for they considerably help in bringing about an adequate supply of labour with skills corresponding to the requirements of product plans.

Inter-occupational differentials may comprise skilled, unskilled and manual wage differentials; non-manual and manual (white and blue-collar); and general skill differentials. Occupational wage differentials generally follow the changes in the relative supplies of labour to various occupations.

Type # 2. Inter-Firm Differentials:

Inter-firm differentials reflect the relative wage levels of workers in different plants in the same area and occupation.

The main causes of inter-firm wage differentials are:

(a) Difference in the quality of labour employed by different firms;

(b) Imperfections in the labour market; and

(c)Differences in the efficiency of equipment, supervision and other non-labour factors.

Differences in technological advance, managerial efficiency, financial capacity, age and size of the firm, relative advantages and disadvantages of supply of raw materials, power and availability of transport facilities — these also account for considerable disparities in inter-firm wage rates. Lack of co-ordination among adjudication authorities, too, is responsible for such anomalies.

Type # 3. Inter-Area or Regional Differentials:

Such differentials arise when workers in the same industry and the same occupational group, but living in different geographical areas, are paid different wages. Regional wage differentials may be conceived in two senses. In the first sense, they are merely a part of inter-industry differentials in a particular region.

"The industry mix varies from one area to another, and for this reason alone, the general average of wages would be expected to vary." 22 In the second sense, they may represent real geographical differentials, resulting in the payment of different rates for the same type of work. In both cases, regional differentials affect the supply of manpower for various plants in different regions.

Such differentials are the result of living and working conditions, such as unsatisfactory or irksome climate, isolation, substandard housing, disparities in the cost of living and the availability of manpower. In some cases, regional differentials are also used to encourage planned mobility of labour.

Type # 4. Inter-Industry Differentials:

These differentials arise when workers in the same occupation and the same area but in different industries are paid different wages. Inter-industry differentials reflect skill differentials. The industries paying higher wages have mostly been industries with a large number of skilled workers, while those paying less have been industries with a large proportion of unskilled and semi-skilled workers.

Other factors influencing inter-industry differentials are the extent of unionisation, the structure of product markets, the ability to pay, labour-capital ratio, and the stage of development of an industry.

Type # 5. Personal Wage Differentials:

These arise because of differences in the personal characteristics (age or sex) of workers who work in the same plant and the same occupation. "Equal pay for equal work" has been recommended by the I.L.O. Convention (No. 100), as also by Industrial Courts, Labour Tribunals, the Minimum Wages Committee and the Fair Wage Committee. But in practice this principle has not been fully implemented because in occupations which involve strenuous muscular work, women workers, if employed, are paid less than men workers.

Lack of organisation among women employees, less mobility among them, their lower subsistence and their weak constitution are other reasons which bring them lower wages than their male counterparts receive.

What is collective bargaining?

Collective bargaining refers to the negotiation of wages and working conditions between workers organizations and employers and/or their organizations. Negotiations as part of collective bargaining take place bilaterally, with government only intervening to create the necessary framework and promote its development.

Collective bargaining can take place at various levels. Under enterprise-level bargaining, each employer bargains independently; under sectoral multi-employer bargaining, employers come together in associations with a mandate to bargain.

The latter type of bargaining is sometimes seen as more inclusive, giving employers and workers more bargaining power and saving on bargaining costs and removing the potentially conflictual topic of pay negotiations from the workplace. This multi-employer type negotiation also establishes a common rule for competition among enterprises that are parties to the agreement. However, it can restrict the independence of individual firms, and may not take into account the heterogeneity of firms within a particular sector. Moreover, many agreements increasingly allow for tailor making of terms at the enterprise level (dual level bargaining) and provide for conditional derogations depending on firm size.

Extension of collective agreements[1] to all enterprises, in accordance with national law and practice, can also be used to ensure fair competition by providing a level playing field and extending coverage to all workers.

Empirical evidence

In many countries, minimum wages and collective bargaining co-exists and complement each other. In principle, minimum wages should be targeted at the lowest-paid employees, while collective bargaining can set wage floors but should also promote wage increases for workers who also earn more than the minimum, in line with productivity growth. However, if the minimum wage is too high or the minimum wage system too complex (with too many rates, including for workers with very different levels of qualifications or occupations), there is a risk that minimum wages will "crowd out" collective bargaining – that is, encroach on the domain of collective bargaining and not leave enough space for the latter to develop.

When collective bargaining is weak, there is a risk that many workers' wages will be clustered around the minimum wage, dragging down median or mean wages.

THEORIES OF INTEREST

Accordingly, there are two concepts of interest. One concept of interest is the real rate of interest which is the rote of retiro on physical capital such as machine, vehicle, tractor created for the purpose of producing more goods. A capital asset is used for production for several years and yields a stream of return over the years. A rate of return on it is obtained by calculating the present discounted value of the yields earned over the number of years for which capital asset is used for production

The second concept of interest is the price paid for the use of borrowed funds from other and is often called money rote of interest These funds are mainly used for investment in physical capital but they may also be used for consumption purposes. It is worth noting that money rate of interest is intimately related to the rate of return on physical capital. When the rate of return on a physical asset, that is, the real rate of interest, is higher than the market money rate of interest, then there will be greater investment in capital with the result that the rate of return on capital will fall. The equilibrium will be established when the rate of retum becomes equal to the money rate of interest.

Classical economists have visualized interest as marginal productivity of physical capital but since physical capital has to be purchased with monetary funds, rate of interest becomes the rate of return over money invested in physical capital. As money to be invested in physical capital has to be saved by someone, interest also becomes the price for abstinence or waiting or time preference involved in the act of saving and lending it to others for investment in capital. There has been no complete agreement among the dassical economists about the nature of interest. Some of them explained interest from the standpoint of the supply side, that , savings, and therefore emphasized the role of abstinence, or waiting or time preference in the determination of interest. On the other

hand, Knight and 1.B. Clark explained the phenomenon of interest only from the viewpoint of the demand for capital and laid stress on the productivity of capital as a determining factor of interest. Irving Fisher, Bohm Bawerk and some others explained the nature and determination of interest taking into account both the time preference (working on the supply side) and the productivity of capital (working on the demand side), it is evident that the classical economists emphasized the role of real factors such as thrift (ie, abstinence or waiting), time preference and productivity of capital in the determination of interest Therefore, the classical theory is also known as real theory of interest.

On the other hand, neo-classical economists such as Wicksell, Ohlin, Haberler, Robertson, Viner etc. developed what is known as Loanable Funds or Neo-Classical Theory of interest. These writers saw the interplay of monetary and non monetary forces in the determination of the rate of interest. At their hands, interest theory ceased to be purely real or non-monetary theory in their view. monetary factors along with the real factors determine the rate of interest. In a way loanable funds theory is a monetary theory of interest

But monetary theory gained more recognition with the publication of Keynes General Theory According to Keynes, interest is purely a monetary phenomenon and as such it is determined by the demand for money (ie, liquidity preference) and the supply of money According to him, interest is à price not for the socrifice of waiting or time preference but for parting with liquidity Since he emphasized the role of liquidity preference in the determination of the interest rate, his theory is known as liquidity preference theory of interest, Keynesian theory is purely a monetary theory.

Some modern economists such as J.R. Hicks, A.P. Lerner and AH Hansen have brought about a synthesis between the classical and neo-classical theories on the one hand and Keynesian liquidity preference theory on the other. We shall discuss all these theories of interest in this chapter. It is worth noting that all these theories of interest seek to explain the determination of the rate of interest through the equilibrium between the forces of demand and supply. In other words, all these theories are demand and supply theories.

The difference between the various theories of interest lies in the answer to the question demand for what and supply of what? According to the classical theory, rate of interest is determined by demand for savings to make investment and the supply of sovings Loanable funds theory seeks to explain the determination of the rate of interest through the equilibrium between demand for and supply of loonable funds Besides savings, loanable funds consist of funds derived from other sources as well. Keynesian theory of interest explains the determination of interest through the equilibrium between the demand for and supply of money

CLASSICAL THEORY OF INTEREST

This theory seeks to explain the determination of the rate of interest through the interaction of the demand for savings to make investment and the supply of savings. Since this theory explains the determination of the rate of interest by real forces such as thrift, time preference and productivity of Capital, it is also called the real theory of interest. Various classical writers differ a good deal from each other in respect of their views about interest. Some of them laid emphasis on the forces governing the supply of savings. Thus they considered interest as a price for abstinence or waiting or

time preference Some others like J.B. Clark and Knight thought the marginal productivity of capital,which is a force that operates on the demand for savings, determines the rate of interest

Fisher and Bohm-Bawerk explained the interest with both types of factors. There is a basic assumption that is common to all classical writers it is that all of them assume full employment of resources. In other words, in their models if more resources are to be devoted to investment, that is,to the production of capital goods, some resources have to be withdrawn from the production of consumer goods

According to this theory, money which is lent out to the entrepreneurs for investment in capital goods is to be made available by those who save out of their incomes. By abstaining from consumption they release resources for the production of capital goods. In order to induce people to save and refrain from consuming a part of their incomes, they must be offered some interest as a reward To persuade them to save more, the higher rate of interest has to be offered. So far the various classical economists agreed but they differed in detail about the nature of interest. We shall discuss below the views of some of them.

INTEREST IS A PRICE FOR ABSTINENCE OR WAITING

It was Nasau Senior who first pointed out that saving involved a sacrifice of abstinence and interest is a price for this sacrifice. Anyone who saves some money and is therefore able to lend it to others abstains from consuming a part of his income and in order to induce him to do so, he must be paid interest by the borrower. Thus, according to Senior, interest arises because of the abstinence involved in the act of saving Without giving him the interest as compensation, the individuals will not like to undergo the sacrifice of abstaining from consumption.

The idea of abstinence was criticized by some economists, in particular by Karl Marx, who pointed out that the rich people who are the main source of savings are able to save without making any real sacrifice of abstinence They save because something is left over after they have indulged in consumption to their heart's desire. In order to avoid this criticism Marshall substituted the word waiting for "abstinence" According to him, when a person saves money and lends it to others, he does not abstain from consumption for all time, he merely postpones consumption. But the individual who lends his savings has to wait until he gets back the money. Thus, the person who saves money and lends it to others undergoes the sacrifice of waiting To induce people to save and wait some price has to be paid to them as compensation for making this sacrifice According to this view, interest is a price for waiting

BOHM BAWERK'S EXPLANATION OF INTEREST

The Austrian economist Bohm-Bawerk put forward another explanation of interest According to him, interest arises because people prefer present goods to future goods of the same kind and quantity and, therefore, there is an agio, or premium on present goods as compared to future goods People prefer present enjoyment to future enjoyment in other words, future satisfaction when viewed from the present undergoes a discount, interest is this discount which must be paid in orde to induce people to lend money and therefore postpone present satisfaction to a future date

BohmBawerk gave three reasons for the emergence of rate of interest.

First, people have relatively greater needs or demands for goods in the present than in the future. In other words, present wants are felt more keenly than the future wants. As a result demand for goods is greater in the present than in the future.

The second reason advanced by Bohm Bawerk is that people underestimate future wants People underestimate future wants because they lack imagination and therefore cannot judge the intensity of their future wants, (i) they lack will and cannot resist the temptation of satisfying present wants and therefore undervalue their future wants, and () the future is uncertain so that they think that they may or may not live to satisfy future wants. In view of all these, people prefer the satisfaction of present wants to future wants Bohm Bawerk describes this as an underestimate of future wants which, according to him, is systematic irrationality

Third reason for the emergence interest given by Bohm Bawerk is what he calls "technical superiority of present over future goods" This is so because the present goods can be used so as to make capital which involves roundabout and time-consuming methods of production and is more productive Because of the greater productivity of capital, people prefer to have present goods which can be used as capital so that they have more goods in the future. They are therefore prepared to pay a premium or agio on the present goods as against future goods and this gives rise to interest

INTEREST IS PAID BECAUSE OF TIME PREFERENCE (FISHER'S THEORY)

Irving Fisher, an eminent American economist, largely accepted Bohm-Bawerk's views about the nature of interest except that he criticised Bohm Bawerk's third ground for interest, that is, the technical superiority of present over future goods. Fisher lays greater emphasis on time preference as a cause of interest But along with time preference he also considered the role of marginal productivity of capital for which he used the term rate of return over cost as a factor that. determines interest.

Rate of interest arises because people preter present satisfaction to future satisfaction. They are therefore impatient to spend their incomes in the present. According to Fisher, interest is a compensation for the time preference of the individual. The greater the impatience to spend money in the present, that is, the greater the preference of individuals for the present enjoyment of goods to future enjoyment of them, the higher will have to be the rate of interest to induce them to lend money

The degree of impatience to spend income in the present depends upon the size of the income the distribution of income over time, the degree of certainty regarding enjoyment in the future and the temperament and character of the individual. The people whose incomes are large are likely to have their present wants more fully satisfied Therefore, these rich people will discount the future at a relatively lower rate of interest (that is their time preference will be less) and will be required to be paid a relatively lower rate of interest.

As regards distribution of income over time, three kinds of situation are possible. The income may be uniform throughout one's life or may increase with age or decrease with age if it is uniform, the degree of impatience to spend in the present will be determined by the size of the income and the temperament of the individual. If the income increases with age, it means the future is well provided for and the degree of impatience to spend money in the present (that is, time preference) will be greater. On the other hand, if the income decreases with age, the degree of patience to spend money at present will be less

As regards certainty of enjoyment in the future, if the individual is sure of enjoyment of income in the future, other things remaining the same, the impatience to spend money in the present will be less, that is, the degree of time preference will be smaller Finally, the character and the temperament of the individual will also determine his time preference. A man of foresight will be less impatient to spend income in the present, that is, his rate of time preference will be less as compared to that of a spendthrift. The rate of time preference is also influenced by expectation of life if a man expects to live long, his preference for spending income in the present will be comparatively low.

It is clear from the analysis that Fisher, like Bohm-Bawerk, regarded the rate of interest as an agio on the present goods exchanged for future goods of the same kind Fisher based his explanation of the rate of interest on his concept of income. According to him, interest is the link between expected future income values and the present capital values based on them. He says, "The value of the orchard depends upon the value of its crops and in this dependence lurks implicitly the rate of interest itself. The statement that 'capital produces income is true only in the physical sense, it is not true in the value sense. On the contrary, income value produces capital value."

DETERMINATION OF THE RATE OF INTEREST IN THE CLASSICAL THEORY

According to the classical theory of interest, rate of interest is determinedthe supply of savings and demand for savings to invest . Some classical economists laid stress on the abstinence or waiting involved in the act of savings and supply of them and some others emphasized the role of time preference as a determinant of the supply savings According to this theory, the money which is to be used for purchasing capital goods is made available by those who save from their current income .By postponing consumption a part of their income they release resources for the production of capital goods

It is assumed in this theory that savings are interest elastic. The higher the rate of interest. the more the savings which people will be induced to make. Besides, at higher rate of interest, savings would be forthcoming from those persons whose rates of time preference are more strongly weighed in favour of present satisfaction. The supply curve of savings will therefore slope upward to the right.

On the other hand, the demand for savings comes from the entrepreneurs or firms which desire to invest in capital goods Capital goods are demanded because they can be used to produce further goods which can be sold to earn income. Thus capital goods have a revenue productivity like all other factors. For any given type of capital asset, eg, a machine, it is possible to draw a marginal revenue productivity curve showing the addition made to total revenue by an additional unit of a machine at various levels of the stock of that machine

✓Like other factors of production, capital has marginal revenue productivity.

√ This net expected return is expressed as percentage of the cost of capital asset. The more capital assets of a given kind there are, the less income will be expected to accrue from a marginal unit of it. Therefore, the marginal revenue productivity curve of capital slopes downward to the right

√ Since the marginal revenue productivity curve of capital slopes downward, it will become profitable to purchase more capital goods as the rate of interest falls, ie.. with the fall in the rate of interest more money will be demanded for investment. Thus, the investment demand curve relating the rate of interest with the investment demand will be downward sloping In other words, investment demand is assumed to be interest elastic.

Determination of Interest

The rate of interest in determined by the equality of demand for capital and supply of capital of saving and investment. In the figure 55 is the supply curve and it is investment curve, which represents demand for capital These two curves intersect at point E. The demand and supply are equal, Rs 60 at point E. Hence, or, 3 percent rate of interest is determined 3 percent is the equilibrium rate of interest.

There cannot be equilibrium at any other rate of interest. As for instance, at 4% rate of interest supply of capital exceeds demand. This will push interest downward, Likewise, at 2% rate of interest demand for capital exceeds supply This will push interest upward Eventually, 3% rate of interest will prevaid in the market if the change occurs either an demand or supply, the demand curve or the supply curve shifts Consequently, there is change in equilibrium rate of interest

LOANABLY FUNDS THEORY OF INTEREST

Another school of thought developed what is called loanable funds theory of interest. Among the principal economists who contributed to the development of loanable funds they may be real forces such as thriltiness, waiting time preference and productivity of capital alone do not go to determine the rate of interest, monetary forces such as hoarding and dishoarding of money, money created by banks, monetary loans for consumption purposes also play a part in the determination of the rate of interest

Thus the exponents of the loanable funds theory saw the interplay of monetary and non-monetary forces in the determination of the rate of interest. Therefore, see that loanable funds theory is a monetary theory of interest, although it is only partly monetary since it also recognises the importance of real forces such as thriftiness and productivity of capital in determination of rate of interest

According to this theory, rate of interest is determined by the demand for and supply of loanable funds. The supply loanable funds consists of savings out of disposable income, dishoarding, money created by the banks and disinvestment (ie, disentangling of fixed and working capital), The demand for loanable funds is composed of demand for investment, demand for consumption and demand for hoarding money

Supply of Loanable Funds

✓ Saving Savings by individuals and households constitute the most important source of the supply of loanable funds in the loanable funds theory savings are considered in either of the two ways. First, in the sense of ex ante saving, that is, savings planned by individuals and households in the beginning of a period in the hope of expected incomes and anticipated expenditures on consumption, and secondly, in the sense of Robertsonian savings, that is the difference between the income of the preceding period (which becomes disposable in the present period) and consumption of the present period in both these senses of savings it is assumed that the amount of savings varies with rate of interest. More savings will be forthcoming at higher rates of interest and vice versa.

It is granted that savings by individuals and households primarily depend upon the size of their income. But, given the level of income, savings vary with the rate of interest, the higher the rate of interest, the greater the volume of savings. Therefore, supply curve of savings slopes upward to the right

√ Dishoarding Dishoarding of the past accumulated savings constitutes another source of supply of loanable funds. Individuals may postess idle cash balances hoarded from the incomes of the previous periods which they may dishoard in a period When people dishoard, the idle cash balances become active cash balances in the present period and thus add to the supply of loanable funds People hoard money because of their preference for liquidity When rate of interest rises or when the prices of bonds and shares decline, they may like to take advantage of these market movements and thus dishoard money for lending it to others or for purchasing bonds and shares. At a higher rate of interest, the individuals possessing idle cash balances will be induced to dishoard more money. At very low rates of interest, their parting with liquidity will not be rewarded sufficiently and, therefore they will hold on to money. It is evident that discarding is interest-elastic and therefore, the curve of discarding slopes upward to the right

✓Bank Money The banking system is another important source of the supply of loanable funds. The commercial banks by creating credit money advance loans to the businessmen and industries for investment Banks can also reduce the supply of loanable funds by contracting their lending Banks also purchase and sell securities and thereby affect the supply of loanable funds The supply curve of funds provided by banks is to some degree interest-elastic Generally speaking, the banks will lend more money at higher rates of interest than at lower ones. Therefore, supply curve of bank money also slopes upward to the right

√ Disinvestment Disinvestment is another source of the supply of loanable funds Disinvestment means disentangling of the present fixed and working capital Usually a good amount of depreciation reserves is kept so as to replace the fixed capital when it is completely worn out. When there is a declining tendency in certain industries due to some structural changes in the economy, the entrepreneurs may not like to remain tied to those industries and therefore they may allow the existing stock of machines and other equipment belonging to those industries wear out without replacement. As a result, they may bring the depreciation reserves in the market for loanable funds Similarly, working capital invested in business may be withdrawn gradually and made available as loanable funds. When disinvestment is decided to be undertaken, then not only the depreciation reserves but also a part of the revenue earned from the sale of output instead of going into capital replacement flows into the market for loanable funds At higher rates of interest, the entrepreneurs will generally contemplate a greater amount of disinvestment Prof. Bober rightly remarks, "Disinvestment is encouraged somewhat by a high rate of interest on Ioanable funds. When the rate is high, some of the current capital may not produce a marginal revenue product to match this rate of interest. The firm may decide to let this capital run down and to put the depreciation funds in the loan market." It is therefore clear that disinvestment curve will also slope upward to the right

Demand for Lonable Funds

Loanable funds theory differs from the classical theory in its explanation of the demand for funds Whereas the classical theory considers only the demand for funds f investment purposes, the anable funds theory also considers the demand of loans for consumption and demand for hoarding oney, apart from the demand of funds for investment.

Investment Demand. Demand for investment constitutes an important factor working on the side of demand for loanable funds. Investment demand includes businessmen's

borrowings for purchasing or making of new capital goods including the building up of inventories. The price of obtaining the loanable funds required to purchase or invest in capital goods is obviously the rate of interest. It will pay businessmen to demand and undertake investment of loanable funds up to the point where the expected net rate of return on investment equals the rate of interest. In the loanable funds theory, demand for investment depends upon the marginal revenue productivity of capital (or the marginal rate of return) in the same way as in the classical theory. When the rate of interest falls businessmen will find it profitable to increase investment in capital goods with the result that their demand for loanable funds will increase. We thus see that demand for loanable funds for investment is interest-elastic; at a low rate of interest, there will be greater investment demand and vice versa. Therefore, the curve of investment demand for loanable funds slopes downward to the right.

Consumption Demand. Another important source of demand for loanable funds are the loans desired to be taken by the people for consumption purposes. Loans for consumption purposes are demanded by the people when they wish to make purchases in excess of their current incomes and idle cash resources. The loans for consumption purposes are demanded generally for buying durable-use goods such as houses, automobiles, refrigerators, television sets, air conditioners etc. Whereas a lower rate of interest will induce people to borrow more for consumption, the higher rate of interest will discourage borrowing for consumption. Therefore, consumption-demand curve for loanable funds slopes downward to the right

√ Demand for Hoarding Lastly, demand for money to hoard is another important factor determining demand for loanable funds. Demand for hoarding money arises because of people's preference for liquidity, se, for cash balances Hoarded money represents idle cash balances People save money when they do not spend all their disposable income on consumption. They can lend out their savings to others or purchase securities (ie. bonds and shares) with their savings or invest their savings in real capital. Another alternative use of income saved (ie, income not spent on consumption) is to hoard them, that is, to hold them as idle cash balances People can also hoard money when they sell securities or assets owned by them and not spending the proceeds obtained therefrom

The ortant thing to understand is why people hoard money when they can earn some income by lending it to others or investing it in securities or capital assets. An important reason for the demand for hoarding money is that people like to take advantage of the changes in the rate of interest or changes in the prices of securities in the future. At higher current rates of interest, people will hoard less money because much of the money will be lent out to take advantage of the higher rates of interest, and people will hoard more money at lower rates of interest because loss suffered in hoarding money in this case will not be very much. It follows therefore that the curve of demand for hoarding money will also slope downward

we have taken the savings (s) on the supply side, dissavings (DS) on the demand side, dishoarding DH) on the supply side and hoarding (H) on the demand side; investment (i) on the demand side and disinvestment on the supply side. We can further simplify our analysis of components of demand for and supply of loanable funds and bring out the conditions the equilibrium rate of terest in a better way if we use net of saving (ie, savings minus dissavings), net of hoarding (e. hoarding minus dishoarding) and net of investment (e investment minus disinvestment).

Theory of Profits.

There is some sort of confusion in the theory of profits due to the lack of agreement among economists about the true or proper function of the entrepreneur. Some have held the view that the section of the entrepreneur is to organize and co-ordinate the other factors of production. According to them, entrepreneur earns profits for his performing this function. On this view, enterprise is a special type of labor and profits a special form of wages. Some others have described the entrepreneur as performing joint and inseparable functions of responsibility (e. ultimate risk bearing) and control (ie, ultimate decision making) The entrepreneur earns profits because he kes a risk of incurring losses when his price and output policies prove to be incorrect in view of the sture business movements. Schumpeter has assigned to the entrepreneur the role of an innovator and profits as a reward for his introducing innovations Lastly, F. H. Knight has emphasized certainty in the economy as a factor which gives rise to profits and bearing of uncertainty is the task of the entrepreneur.

Besides, some economists have described profits as non-functional income. Thus 1.M. Keynes expressed the view that profits resulted from the favorable movements of the general price level. loan Robinson, E.H. Chamberlin and M. Kalecki have associated profits with the imperfect competition and monopoly. According to them, the greater the degree of imperfection or, in other words, the greater the degree of monopoly power, the greater the profits made by the entrepreneur. Thus, profit has been associated by F. H. Knight with uncertainty. by Schumpeter with inovations, by Hawley with risk-bearing, and by Joan Robinson EH. Chamberlin and M. Kalecki with the degree of monopoly power. As a matter of fact, profits arise from all these sources

Therefore, no single explanation or theory of profits is adequate; each omits some crucial factors and fails to bring out some important economic phenomena having a relation with profits. Prof. 8:5 Keirstead, therefore, expresses the view that profits originate from monopoly, successful innovation and a correct estimate of uncertain future. He thus says, "Profits may come to exist as a result of monopoly or monopsony, as a reward for innovation, as a reward for the correct estimate of uncertain factors, either particular to the industry or general to the whole economy"

PROFIT AS A DYNAMIC SURPLUS

A popular conception of profits is that they arise in a dynamic economy, that is in an economy where changes are taking place in a static economy where nothing changes there can be no profits It was 18 Clark who first propounded that profits are a dynamic surplus. He argued that in a stationary state where no changes in conditions of demand and supply are occurring, the prices paid to the factors on the basis of their marginal productivity would exhaust the total value production and no profits would accrue to the entrepreneur result when selling prices of the goods exceed their cast of production in a competitive long run equilibrium, price equals average cost of production (including normal profits which are in fact wages for routine supervision and management) and therefore no pure profits are made. Now, if no changes esther in the conditions of demand or in the conditions of supply occur, competitive equilibrium will persist and therefore no profits will be earned by the entrepreneur On the contrary, if due to the changes in either demand or supply, price exceeds cost of production, profits will emerge. if due to these changes, price falls below the cost of production, negative profits, that is, losses, will accrue to the entrepreneur. It is evident that changes disturb the equilibrium and thereby give rise to profits

Clark mentioned five changes that occur in a dynamic economy and which give rise to profits. These five changes are

- changes in the quantity and quality of human wants,
- changes in methods or techniques of production,
- changes in the amount of capital and
- changes in the forms of business organization,

These changes are constantly taking place and bring about the divergence between price and cost thereby give rise to profits, positive or negative if the demand for a commodity increases due to the increase in population or increase in the incomes of the people or due to the increase in consumers preference for the commodity, the price of the commodity will rise, and if cost remains the same, profits would accrue to the entrepreneurs producing the commodity. On the other hand, cost of production may go down as a result of the adoption of a new technique of production, or as a result of cheapening of the raw material, and if price remains constant or does not fall to the same extent, the profits would emerge

Apart from the five changes mentioned by Clark, there are other changes also which occur in the economy. All the changes which take place and as a result of which profits arise in a dynamic conomy may be classified into two types:

(1) innovations and

(2) exogenous changes

Innovations represent changes which are introduced by individual entrepreneurs themselves. The entrepreneur earns large profits from introducing innovations such as a new product, a new and cheaper method of production, a new method of marketing the product, a new way of advertisement. The innovational changes may either reduce cost or increase the demand for the product and thereby bring profits into existence. Those entrepreneurs who introduce successful innovations earn farge profits

Exogenous changes refer to those changes which are external to the firms or industries in an economy. These changes affect all firms in an industry or sometimes all the industries in the economy Examples of exogenous changes are breaking out of wars, occurrence of sometimes periods of inflation and rising prices and sometimes business depression and falling prices, changes in the monetary and fiscal policies of government affecting favorably or unfavorably, changes in the technology of production changes in tastes and preferences of the consumers, changes in income. and spending habits of the people, changes in the availability of substitute products, alteration in the egislative and legal environment affecting the industries, and changes in preferences between ncome and leisure All these changes affect either the cost or demand of the products and give rise profits, positive or negative as the case may be far instance, during war when prices of goods mount up, and costs lag behind, the entrepreneurs make a lot of profits Similarly, when inflation occurs due to the increased demand for goods caused rising incomes, increasing population and exparision in the money supply, the huge profits accrue the firms. On the contrary, when period of depression comes due to the fall in effective aggregate demand, firms suffer huge losses and some may go into liquidation During periods of depression, all kes, rents, wages, and interest tend to fall but because of the non-contractual nature, profits fall arply and even become negative.

NOVATIONS AND PROFITS: SCHUMPETER'S THEORY OF PROFITS

Schumpeter attributes profit to dynamic changes resulting from an innovation. To start with takes a capitalist closed economy which is in a stationary equilibrium. This equilibrium is aracterised by what Schumpeter calls a "circular flow" which continues to repeat itself for ever in th a static state, there is perfectly competitive equilibrium. The price of each product just equals cost of production and there is no profit.

innovation? Innovation, as used by Schumpeter, has a very wide " connotation. Any new mand for his product is an innovation. Thus, innovation has two categories

First type of innovations are those which reduce cost of production, or in other words, which change the production functions in this first type of innovations are included the introduction of a new machinery, new and cheaper technique or process of production exploitation of a new source of raw material, a new and better method of organizing the firm, etc.

Second type of innovations are those which increase the demand for the product, or in other words, which change the demand or utility function to this category are included the introduction of a new product, a new variety or design of the product, a new and superior method of advertisement, discovery of new markets etc.

If an innovation proves successful, that is, if it achieves its aim of either reducing the cost of production or enhancing the demand for the product, it will give rise to profit. Profits emerge because due to successful innovation either cost falls below the prevailing price of the product or the entrepreneur is able to sell z more and at a better price than before. It should be noted that profits accrue not to him who concelves innovation nor to him who finances it but to him who introduces it. Further, whenever any new innovation is contemplated to be introduced, it always calls for a new combination of factors or reallocation of resources

it is here worth mentioning that profits caused by a particular innovation are only temporary and tend to be competed away as others imitate and also adopt that. An innovation ceases to be new or novel, when others also come to know of it and adopt it. When an entrepreneur introduces a new innovation, he is first in a monopoly position, for the new innovation is confined to him only He therefore makes large profits. When after some time others also adopt it in order to get a share, profits will disappear. If the law allows and the entrepreneur is able to get his new innovation, eg. new product patented, then he will continue to earn profits

THE RISK THEORY

The risk theory of profit is associated with FB Hawley who regards risk taking as the main function of the entrepreneur Profit is the residual income which the entrepreneur receives for the reason that he assumes risks. The entrepreneur exposes his business to risk and receives in turn a reward in the form of profit since the task of risk taking is infuriating Profit is an excess of payment above the actuarial value of risk. No entrepreneur will be willing to undertake risks if he gets only the normal return. Hence the reward for risk taking must be higher than the actual value of risk.

THE UNCERTAINTY BEARING THEORY

Prof Frank H knight regards profit as the reward of bearing non insurable risks and uncertainties. He distinguishes amidst insurable and non-insurable risks. Certain risks are measurable in as much as the probability of their occurrence can be statistically calculated. The risk of fire theft of merchandise and of death by accident is insurable. Such risks are borne by the insurance company There are certain unique risks which are incalculable. The probability of their occurrence cannot be statistically computed for the reason that of the presence of uncertainty in them.

Such unforeseen risks relate to changes in prices, demand and supply etc. No insurance company can calculate the loss expected from such risks and hence they are non-insurable Profit according to Knight is the reward of bearing non-insurable risks and uncertainties. It is a deviation arising from uncertainty between earning ex post and ex ante

SHACKLE'S THEORY

Prof GLS Shackle has extended Knight's theory of profit by introducing expectations under conditions of uncertainty. According to him, expectations are of two types: general and particular General expectations relate to variables general to the economy as a whole. They are associated with such micro variables as the future reaction of a particular marketing strategy adopted by a firm, the future pricing policy of a competitive firm etc.

The decisions of the business community are generally based on general expectations. If it regards them favourable investments are made. But there is subjective certainty in the case of general expectations. Their time horizon is about 12 months. As the general expectations have subjective certainty and their time horizon is also of reasonable duration, the business community is able to anticipate price and income increases correctly for the economy as a whole and by adopting appropriate inventory policies it earns windfall profit

RENT THEORY OF PROFIT

The rent theory was developed by an American economist Francis L Walker. Walker maintains that profit is the rent of ability. Like different grades of land, entrepreneurs are also of different abilities. Entrepreneurs of superior ability earn profit just as superior lands earn rent According to Walker just as there is the marginal or no rent land, similarly there exists a marginal or no profit entrepreneur who earns only wages only wages of management. The marginal or no profit entrepreneur is the least efficient one earning profit not beyond an amount just sufficient to keep him in his present industry. The industry managed by the marginal entrepreneur is similar to the marginal land. Just as land at the margin is no rent land, similarly the marginal entrepreneur earns no profit.

Economics is popularly known as the "Queen of Social Sciences". It studies economic activities of a man living in a society. Economic activities are those activities, which are concerned with the efficient use of scarce means that can satisfy the wants of man. After the basic needs viz., food, shelter and clothing have been satisfied, the priorities shift towards other wants. Human wants are unlimited, in the sense, that as soon as one want is satisfied another crops up. Most of the means of satisfying these wants are limited, because their supply is less than demand. These means have alternative uses; there emerge a problem of choice. Resources being scarce in nature ought to be utilized productively within the available means to derive maximum satisfaction. The knowledge of economics guides us in making effective decisions. The subject matter of economics is concerned with wants, efforts and satisfaction. In other words, it deals with decisions regarding the commodities and services to be produced in the economy, how to produce them most economically and how to provide for the growth of the economy.

Printed by Libri Plureos GmbH in Hamburg,
Germany